CORNERSTONES
FOR COLLEGE SUCCESS
COMPACT

Robert M. Sherfield
College of Southern Nevada

Patricia G. Moody
University of South Carolina

Boston • Columbus • Indianapolis • New York • San Francisco • Upper Saddle River
Amsterdam • Cape Town • Dubai • London • Madrid • Milan • Munich • Paris • Montreal • Toronto
Delhi • Mexico City • São Paulo • Sydney • Hong Kong • Seoul • Singapore • Taipei • Tokyo

Editor-in-Chief: Jodi McPherson
Acquisitions Editor: Katie Mahan
Managing Editor: Karen Wernholm
Associate Managing Editor: Tamela Ambush
Senior Development Editor: Shannon Steed
Editorial Assistant: Erin Carreiro
Senior Production Project Manager: Peggy McMahon
Senior Procurement Specialist: Megan Cochran
Editorial Production Service: Electronic Publishing Services Inc.
Electronic Composition: Jouve
Interior Design: Electronic Publishing Services Inc.
Cover Designer: Barbara T. Atkinson
Associate Director of Design, USHE EMSS/HSC/EDU: Andrea Nix
Executive Marketing Manager: Amy Judd
Image Manager: Rachel Youdelman
Permissions Manager: Carol Besenjak
Permissions Project Manager: Pam Foley

Credits and acknowledgments borrowed from other sources and reproduced, with permission, in this textbook appear on the appropriate page within text.

Many of the designations used by manufacturers and sellers to distinguish their products are claimed as trademarks. Where those designations appear in this book, and Pearson Education was aware of a trademark claim, the designations have been printed in initial caps or all caps.

Library of Congress Cataloging-in-Publication Data
Sherfield, Robert M.
  Cornerstones for college success compact / Robert M. Sherfield, Patricia G. Moody.
    p. cm.
  Includes bibliographical references and index.
  ISBN-13: 978-0-321-86035-4
  ISBN-10: 0-321-86035-7
  1. College student orientation—United States.   I. Moody, Patricia G.   II. Title.
  LB2343.32.S54 2013
  378.1'98—dc23

                                                                2012021577

2 3 4 5 6 7 8 9 10—V011—15 14 13

ISBN 10: 0-321-86035-7
ISBN 13: 978-0-321-86035-4

ABOUT YOUR AUTHORS

ROBERT M. SHERFIELD, PH.D.

Robert Sherfield has been teaching public speaking, theater, technical writing, and student success, as well as working with first-year success programs for over 25 years. Currently, he is a professor at the College of Southern Nevada, teaching student success, professional communication, and drama.

An award-winning educator, Sherfield was named Educator of the Year at the College of Southern Nevada. He twice received the Distinguished Teacher of the Year Award from the University of South Carolina at Union, and has received numerous other awards and nominations for outstanding classroom instruction and advisement.

He has extensive experience with the design and implementation of student success programs, including one that was presented at the International Conference on the First-Year Experience in Newcastle upon Tyne, England. He has conducted faculty development keynotes and workshops at over 400 institutions of higher education across the United States. He has spoken in 46 states and several foreign countries.

In addition to his coauthorship of *Cornerstones for Community College Success* (Pearson, 2012), he has authored or coauthored *Cornerstones for Professionalism* (Pearson, 2013), *Cornerstones for Career College Success* (Pearson, 2013), *Cornerstone: Discovering Your Potential, Learning Actively, and Living Well* (Prentice Hall, 2008), *Roadways to Success* (Prentice Hall, 2001), the trade book *365 Things I Learned in College* (Allyn & Bacon, 1996), *Capstone: Succeeding Beyond College* (Prentice Hall, 2001), *Case Studies for the First Year: An Odyssey into Critical Thinking and Problem Solving* (Prentice Hall, 2004), and *The Everything Self-Esteem Book* (Adams Media, 2004).

Sherfield's interest in student success began with his own first year in college. Low SAT scores and a dismal high school ranking denied him entrance into college. With the help of a success program, Sherfield was granted entrance into college and went on to earn five college degrees, including a doctorate. He has always been interested in the social, academic, and cultural development of students, and sees this book as his way to help students enter the world of work and establish lasting, rewarding careers. Visit www.robertsherfield.com.

PATRICIA G. MOODY, PH.D.

Patricia G. Moody is Dean Emerita of the College of Hospitality, Retail, and Sport Management at the University of South Carolina, where she has served on the faculty and in administration for over 30 years. An award-winning educator, Moody was honored as Distinguished Educator of the Year at her college and as Collegiate Teacher of the Year by the National Business Education Association. She was also a top-five finalist for the Amoco Teaching Award at the University of South Carolina. She received the prestigious John Robert Gregg Award, the highest honor in her field of over 100,000 educators.

Moody has coauthored many texts and simulations, including *Cornerstones for Professionalism* (Pearson, 2013), *Cornerstones for Career College Success* (Pearson, 2013), *Cornerstones for Community College Success* (Pearson, 2012), *Cornerstone: Discovering Your Potential, Learning Actively, and Living Well* (Prentice Hall, 2008), *365 Things I Learned in College* (Allyn & Bacon, 1996), *Capstone: Succeeding Beyond College* (Prentice Hall, 2001), and *Case Studies for the First Year: An Odyssey into Critical Thinking and Problem Solving* (Prentice Hall, 2004).

A nationally known motivational speaker, consultant, and author, Moody has spoken in most states, has been invited to speak in several foreign countries, and frequently keynotes national and regional conventions. She has presented her signature motivational keynote address, "Fly Like an Eagle," to tens of thousands of people, from Olympic athletes to corporate executives to high school students.

As the dean of her college, Moody led international trips to build relationships and establish joint research projects in hospitality. Under her direction, faculty members in her college began a landmark study of Chinese tourists. She now travels the country delivering workshops, keynotes, and presentations on topics such as Managing Change, Working in the New Global Community, the Future of the Future, Student Motivation, and Emotional Intelligence. Moody also serves as a personal coach for business executives.

MyStudentSuccessLab is an online solution designed to help students acquire the skills they need to succeed for ongoing personal and professional development. They will have access to peer-led video interviews and develop core skills through interactive practice exercises and activities that provide academic, life, and professionalism skills that will transfer to ANY course.

How can "skills" be measured – and what can you do with the data?

Measurement Matters – and is ongoing in nature. No one is ever an "expert" in 'soft skills' - something students learn once and never think about again. They take these skills with them for life.

Learning Path Diagnostic

- For the course, 65 Pre-Course questions (Levels I & II Bloom's) and 65 Post-Course questions (Levels III & IV Bloom's) that link to key learning objectives in each topic.

- For each topic, 20 Pre-Test questions (Levels I & II Bloom's) and 20 Post-Test questions (Levels III & IV Bloom's) that link to all learning objectives in the topic.

What gets your attention?

It's about engagement. Everyone likes videos.
Good videos, conveniently organized by topic.

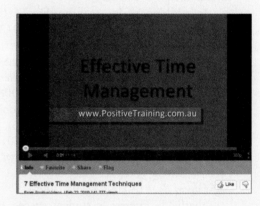

FinishStrong247 YouTube channel

- Best of 'how to' for use as a practical reference
  (i.e. - manage your priorities using a smart phone)

- Save time finding good video.

- All videos have been approved by members of our student advisory board and peer reviewed.

How can everyone get trained?

We all want a 'shortcut to implementation'.
Instructors want to save time on course prep.
Students want to know how to register, log in, and know 'what's due, and when'.
We can make it easy.

Implementation Guide

- Organized by topic, provides time on task, grading rubrics, suggestions for video use, and more.

- Additional videos and user guides, registration and log in guides, and technical support for instructors and students at www.mystudentsuccesslab.com

MyStudentSuccessLab
Start Strong. Finish Stronger.
www.MyStudentSuccessLab.com

MyStudentSuccessLab Feature set:

Learning Path provides:
- 65 Pre-Course (Levels I & II Bloom's) and 65 Post-Course (Levels III & IV Bloom's)
- 20 Pre-Test (Levels I & II Bloom's) and 20 Post-Test (Levels III & IV Bloom's)
- Overview (ie. – Learning Outcomes)
- Student Video Interviews (with Reflection questions)
- Practices and Activities Tied to Learning Path
- FinishStronger247 YouTube channel with student vetted supporting videos

Student Inventories:
1. **Golden Personality**—Similar to Meyers Briggs–it offers a personality assessment and robust reporting for students to get actionable insights on personal style. **www. talentlens.com/en/employee-assessments/golden.php**
2. **ACES (Academic Competence Evaluation Scales)**—Strength inventory which identifies and screens students to help educators prioritize skills and provides an overview of how students see themselves as learners. Identifies at-risk. **www.pearsonassessments.com/HAIWEB/Cultures/en-us/ Productdetail.htm?Pid=015-8005-805**
3. **(Watson-Glaser) Thinking Styles**—Helps students understand their thought process and how they tend to approach situations. Shows how you make decisions. **www.thinkwatson.com/mythinkingstyles**

Student Resources:
Pearson Students Facebook page, FinishStrong247 YouTube channel, MySearchLab, Online Dictionary, Plagiarism Guide, Student Planner, MyProfessionalismKit resources including video cases, job search documents, and interview FAQ's. GPA, Savings, Budgeting, and Retirement Calculators.

Instructor Resources:
Instructor Implementation Guide supports course prep with Overview, Time on Task, Grading rubric, etc.

MyStudentSuccessLab Topic List:

A First Step: Goal Setting	Memory and Studying
Communication	Problem Solving
Critical Thinking	Reading and Annotating
Financial Literacy	Stress Management
Information Literacy	Teamwork
Interviewing	Test Taking
Job Search Strategies	Time Management
Learning Preferences	Workplace Communication (formerly 'Professionalism')
Listening and Taking Notes in Class	Workplace Etiquette
Majors/Careers and Resumes	

MyLabsPlus Available upon request for MyStudentSuccessLab

mylabsplus MyLabsPlus service is a dynamic online teaching and learning environment designed to support online instruction programs with rich, engaging customized content. With powerful administrator tools and dedicated support, MyLabsPlus is designed to support growing online instruction programs with an advanced suite of management tools. Working in conjunction with MyLabs and Mastering content and technology, schools can quickly and easily integrate MyLabsPlus into their curriculum.

Student Success CourseConnect

Student Success CourseConnect (http://www.pearsonlearningsolutions.com/courseconnect) is one of many award-winning CourseConnect customizable online courses designed by subject matter experts and credentialed instructional designers, and helps students 'Start strong, Finish stronger' by building skills for ongoing personal and professional development.

Topic-based interactive modules follow a consistent learning path, from Introduction, to Presentation, to Activity, then Review. Student Success CourseConnect is available in your school's learning management system (LMS) and includes relevant video, audio, and activities. Syllabi, discussion forum topics and questions, assignments, and quizzes are easily accessible and it accommodates various term lengths as well as self-paced study.

Course Outline (ie 'Lesson Plans')

1. Goal setting, Values, and Motivation
2. Time Management
3. Financial Literacy
4. Creative Thinking, Critical Thinking, and Problem Solving
5. Learning Preferences
6. Listening and Note-Taking in Class
7. Reading and Annotating
8. Studying, Memory, and Test-Taking
9. Communicating and Teamwork
10. Information Literacy
11. Staying Balanced: Stress Management
12. Career Exploration

10. In what ways do you see today's mathematics connected to your everyday life?

"What makes my CourseConnect course so successful is all the engagement that is built-in for students. My students really benefit from the videos, and all the interactivity that goes along with the classes that I've designed for them."

—Kelly Kirk, Director of Distance Education, Randolph Community College

"It's truly great that Pearson is invested in using the latest technologies to reach me in ways beside the traditional educational model. This innovative approach is one of the best ways to facilitate the education of students of my generation."

—Zach Gonzales, Student, University of Denver

Resources for Online Learning or Hybrid

Power Up: A Practical Student's Guide to Online Learning, 2/e

Barrett / Poe / Spagnola-Doyle

©2012 • ISBN-10: 0132788195 • ISBN-13: 9780132788199

Serves as a textbook for students of all backgrounds who are new to online learning and as a reference book for instructors who are also novices in the area, or who need insight into the perspective of such students. Provides readers with the knowledge and practice they need to be successful online learners.

"We have used this excellent text with all cohorts of the last two years, as the text is an integral part of the first course in our graduate online program. Students love that its user-friendly and practical. Instructors see this text as a powerful learning tool that is concise yet is able to be comprehensive in its coverage of critical skills and knowledge that support online student success."

—Dr. William Prado
Associate Professor & Director,
Business Program, Green Mountain College

CourseSmart is the Smarter Way

To learn for yourself, visit
www.coursesmart.com

Introducing CourseSmart, The world's largest online marketplace for digital texts and course materials.

A Smarter Way for Students

CourseSmart is convenient. Students have instant access to exactly the materials their instructor assigns.

CourseSmart offers choice. With CourseSmart, students have a high-quality alternative to the print textbook.

CourseSmart saves money. CourseSmart digital solutions can be purchased for up to 50% less than traditional print textbooks.

CourseSmart offers education value. Students receive the same content offered in the print textbook enhanced by the search, notetaking, and printing tools of a web application.

Resources

Online Instructor's Manual – This manual is intended to give instructors a framework or blueprint of ideas and suggestions that may assist them in providing their students with activities, journal writing, thought-provoking situations, and group activities.

Online PowerPoint Presentation – A comprehensive set of PowerPoint slides that can be used by instructors for class presentations and also by students for lecture preview or review. The PowerPoint Presentation includes bullet point slides with overview information for each chapter. These slides help students understand and review concepts within each chapter.

Assessment via MyStudentSuccessLab – It is an online solution—*and powerful assessment tool*—designed to help students build the skills they need to succeed for ongoing personal and professional development at www.mystudentsuccesslab.com

Create tests using a secure testing engine within MyStudentSuccessLab (similar to Pearson MyTest) to print or deliver online. The high quality and volume of test questions allows for data comparison and measurement which is highly sought after and frequently required from institutions.

- Quickly create a test within MyStudentSuccessLab for use online or to save to Word or PDF format and print

- Draws from a rich library of question test banks that complement course learning outcomes

- Like the option in former test managers (MyTest and TestGen), test questions in MyStudentSuccessLab are organized by learning outcome

- On National average, Student Success materials are customized by 78% of instructors—in both sequence and depth of materials, so organizing by learning outcomes (as opposed to 'chapter') saves customers time

- Questions that test specific learning outcomes in a text chapter are easy to find by using the ACTIVITIES/ASSESSMENTS MANAGER in MyStudentSuccessLab

- MyStudentSuccessLab allows for personalization with the ability to edit individual questions or entire tests to accommodate specific teaching needs

- Because MyStudentSuccessLab is written to learning outcomes, this technology has breadth across any course where 'soft skills' are being addressed

LASSI – The LASSI is a 10-scale, 80-item assessment of students' awareness about and use of learning and study strategies. Addressing skill, will and self-regulation, the focus is on both covert and overt thoughts, behaviors, attitudes and beliefs that relate to successful learning and that can be altered through educational interventions.

Noel Levitz/RMS – This retention tool measures Academic Motivation, General Coping Ability, Receptivity to Support Services, PLUS Social Motivation. It helps identify at-risk students, the areas with which they struggle, and their receptiveness to support.

Premier Annual Planner – This specially designed, annual 4-color collegiate planner includes an academic planning/resources section, monthly planning section (2 pages/month), and weekly planning section (48 weeks; July start date). The Premier Annual Planner facilitates short-term as well as long-term planning. This text is spiral bound and convenient to carry with a 6x9 inch trim size.

Custom Publishing

As the industry leader in custom publishing, we are committed to meeting your instructional needs by offering flexible and creative choices for course materials that will maximize learning and engagement of students.

The Pearson Custom Library

Using our online book-building system, www.pearsoncustomlibrary.com, create a custom book by selecting content from our course-specific collections which consist of chapters from Pearson Student Success and Career Development titles and carefully selected, copyright cleared, third-party content, and pedagogy.
www.pearsonlearningsolutions.com/custom-library/pearson-custom-student-success-and-career-development

Custom Publications

In partnership with your Custom Field Editor, modify, adapt and combine existing Pearson books by choosing content from across the curriculum and organize it around your learning outcomes. As an alternative, work with them to develop your original material and create a textbook that meets your course goals.
www.pearsonlearningsolutions.com/custom-publications

Custom Technology Solutions

Work with Pearson's trained professionals, in a truly consultative process, to create engaging learning solutions. From interactive learning tools to eTexts, to custom websites and portals we'll help you simplify your life as an instructor.
www.pearsonlearningsolutions.com/higher-education/customizable-technology-resources.php

Online Education

Offers online course content for online learning classes, hybrid courses, and enhances the traditional classroom. Our award-winning product CourseConnect includes a fully developed syllabus, media-rich lecture presentations, audio lectures, a wide variety of assessments, discussion board questions, and a strong instructor resource package.
www.pearsonlearningsolutions.com/higher-education/customizable-online-courseware.php

For more information on how Pearson Custom Student Success can work for you, please visit **www.pearsonlearningsolutions.com** or call 800-777-6872

ALWAYS LEARNING

PEARSON

ACKNOWLEDGMENTS and GRATITUDE

We would like to thank the following individuals at **The College of Southern Nevada** for their support:

Dr. Michael Richards, President
Dr. Darren Divine, Vice President for Academic Affairs
Dr. Hyla Winters, Associate Vice President for Academic Affairs
Dr. Levia Hayes, Department Chair–English
Dr. Kathy Baker, Assistant Chair–English
Professor Linda Gannon, Lead Faculty, College Success

We would also like to thank individuals at **The University of South Carolina** and faculty members in the College of Hospitality, Retail, and Sport Management.

To the **amazing individuals** who shared their life stories with us for the feature *From Ordinary to Extraordinary: Real People. Real Lives. Real Change.*

Luke Bryan
Vivian Wong
Leo G. Borges
Dr. Wayne A. Jones
Sylvia Eberhardt
Dino Gonzalez, M.D.
Lydia Hausler Lebovic
H.P. Rama
Derwin Wallace
Matt Karres
Mark Jones

We offer our sincere thanks to the members of our **Cornerstones Advisory Council** who have provided valuable ideas and guidance throughout the development and revision of this title:

Emily Battaglia, *UEI Colleges*
Glenn F. Corillo, Ph.D., *ECPI University*
Patricia Davis, Houston Community College/Southwest
Steve Forshier, *M.Ed.,R.T.(R), Pima Medical Institute*
Michelle Kloss, *South University*
Zachary Lesak, *Miller-Motte Technical College, North Charleston, SC*
Ashley Hailston McMillion, *Daymar Colleges Group*
Adam Oldach, *Western Governors University*
Anthony Siciliano, *Western Governors University*
Zachary Stahmer, *Anthem Education Group*

LaToya L. Trowers, *MBA, CMAA, CPM, COM, Mildred Elley College–NYC Metro Campus*
Lori Ebert, *Brown Mackie College*

Reviewers for this new edition and previous editions of *Cornerstones* whom we recognize with deep appreciation and gratitude:

Elvira Johnson, Central Piedmont Community College; Ryan Messatzzia, Wor-Wic Community College; Sarah K. Shutt, J. Sergeant Reynolds Community College; Kristina Leonard, Daytona Beach College; Kim Long, Valencia Community College; Taunya Paul, York Technical College; Charlie L. Dy, Northern Virginia Community College; Gary H. Wanamamker, Houston Community College; Jo Ann Jenkins, Moraine Valley Community College; Judith Lynch, Kansas State University; Timothy J. Quezada, El Paso Community College; Cathy Hall, Indiana University NW; Beverly J. Slaughter, Brevard Community College; Peg Adams, Northern Kentucky University; Sheryl Duquette, Erie Community College; Melanie Deffendall, Delgado Community College; Arthur Webb, Oklahoma State University; Stephanie Young, Butler Community College; Tara Wertz, MTI College; Diana Clennan, College of Southern Nevada; Jennifer Huss-Basquiat, College of Southern Nevada; Wayne A. Jones, Virginia State University; Barbara Auris, Montgomery County Community College, Betty Fortune, Houston Community College; Joel V. McGee, Texas A & M University; Jan Norton, University of Wisconsin–Osh Kosh; Todd Phillips, East Central College; Christian M. Blum, Bryan and Stratton College; James Briski, Katherine Gibbs School; Pela Selene Terry, Art Institute of NYC; Christina Donnelly, York Technical College; Connie Egelman, Nassau Community College; Amy Hickman, Collins College; Beth Humes, Pennsylvania Culinary Institute; Kim Joyce, Art Institute of Philadelphia; Lawrence Ludwig, Sanford-Brown College; Bethany Marcus, ECPI College of Technology; Kate Sawyer, Pittsburgh Technical Institute; Patricia Sell, National College of Business and Technology; Janis Stiewing, PIMA Medical Institute; June Sullivan, Florida Metropolitan University; Fred Amador, Phoenix College; Kathy Bryan, Daytona Beach Community College; Dorothy Chase, Community College of Southern Nevada; JoAnn Credle, Northern Virginia Community College; Betty Fortune, Houston Community College; Doroteo Franco Jr., El Paso Community College; Cynthia Garrard, Massasoit Community College; Joel Jessen, Eastfield College; Peter Johnston, Massasoit Community College; Steve Konowalow, Community College of Southern Nevada; Janet Lindner, Midlands Technical

College; Carmen McNeil, Solano College; Joan O'Connor, New York Institute of Technology; Mary Pepe, Valencia Community College; Bennie Perdue, Miami-Dade Community College; Ginny Peterson-Tennant, Miami-Dade Community College; Anna E. Ward, Miami-Dade Community College; Wistar M. Withers, Northern Virginia Community College; Marie Zander, New York Institute of Technology; Joanne Bassett, Shelby State Community College; Sandra M. Bovain-Lowe, Cumberland Community College; Carol Brooks, GMI Engineering and Management Institute; Elaine H. Byrd, Utah Valley State College; Janet Cutshall, Sussex County Community College; Deborah Daiek, Wayne State University; David DeFrain, Central Missouri State University; Leslie L. Duckworth, Florida Community College at Jacksonville; Marnell Hayes, Lake City Community College; Elzora Holland, University of Michigan, Ann Arbor; Earlyn G. Jordan, Fayetteville State University; John Lowry-King, Eastern New Mexico University; Charlene Latimer; Michael Laven, University of Southwestern Louisiana; Judith Lynch, Kansas State University; Susan Magun-Jackson, The University of Memphis; Charles William Martin, California State University, San Bernardino; Jeffrey A. Miller; Ronald W. Johnsrud, Lake City Community College; Joseph R. Krzyzanowski, Albuquerque PIMA Medical Institute; June Sullivan, Florida Metropolitan University; Fred Amador, Phoenix College; Kathy Bryan, Daytona Beach Community College; Dorothy Chase, Community College of Southern Nevada; JoAnn Credle, Northern Virginia Community College; Betty Fortune, Houston Community College; Doroteo Franco Jr., El Paso Community College; Cynthia Garrard, Massasoit Community College; Joel Jessen, Eastfield College; Peter Johnston, Massasoit Community College; Steve Konowalow, Community College of Southern Nevada; Janet Lindner, Midlands Technical College; Carmen McNeil, Solano College; Joan O'Connor, New York Institute of Technology; Mary Pepe, Valencia Community College; Bennie Perdue, Miami-Dade Community College; Ginny Peterson-Tennant, Miami-Dade Community College; Anna E. Ward, Miami-Dade Community College; Wistar M. Withers, Northern Virginia Community College; Marie Zander, New York Institute of Technology; Joanne Bassett, Shelby State Community College; Sandra M. Bovain-Lowe, Cumberland Community College; Carol Brooks, GMI Engineering and Management Institute; Elaine H. Byrd, Utah Valley State College; Janet Cutshall, Sussex County Community College; Deborah Daiek, Wayne State University; David DeFrain, Central Missouri State University; Leslie L. Duckworth, Florida Community College at Jacksonville; Marnell Hayes, Lake City Community College; Elzora Holland, University of Michigan, Ann Arbor; Earlyn G. Jordan, Fayetteville State University; John Lowry-King, Eastern New Mexico University; Charlene Latimer; Michael Laven, University of Southwestern

Louisiana; Judith Lynch, Kansas State University; Susan Magun-Jackson, The University of Memphis; Charles William Martin, California State University, San Bernardino; Jeffrey A. Miller; Ronald W. Johnsrud, Lake City Community College; Joseph R. Krzyzanowski, Albuquerque TVI; Ellen Oppenberg, Glendale Community College; Lee Pelton, Charles S. Mott Community College; Robert Rozzelle, Wichita State University; Penny Schempp, Western Iowa Community College; Betty Smith, University of Nebraska at Kearney; James Stepp, University of Maine at Presque Isle; Charles Washington, Indiana University–Purdue University; Katherine A. Wenen-Nesbit, Chippewa Valley Technical College; Kristina Leonard, Daytona Beach College; Kim Long, Valencia Community College; Taunya Paul, York Technical College; Charlie L. Dy, Northern Virginia Community College; Gary H. Wanamamker, Ph. D., Houston Community College; Jo Ann Jenkins, Moraine Valley Community College; Judith Lynch, Kansas State University; Timothy J. Quezada, El Paso Community College; Cathy Hall, Indiana University NW; Beverly J. Slaughter, Brevard Community College; Peg Adams, Northern Kentucky University; Sheryl Duquette, Erie Community College; Melanie Deffendall, Delgado Community College; Arthur Webb, Oklahoma State University; Stephanie Young, Butler Community College; Tara Wertz, MTI College; Diana Clennan, College of Southern Nevada; Jennifer Huss-Basquiat, College of Southern Nevada; Wayne A. Jones, Virginia State University; Pamela Stephens, Fairmont State University; and Angela Vaughan, University of Northern Colorado.

Our Creative and Supportive Team at Pearson Education

Without the support and encouragement of the following people at Pearson Education, this book would not be possible. Our sincere thanks to:

Jodi McPherson
Amy Judd
Katie Mahan
Shannon Steed
Peggy McMahon

Your constant belief in us has been a most cherished gift. We are lucky to know you and are better people because of you. Thank you!

We also thank the following friends at Pearson for their support, dedication, and exceptional work: Erin Carreiro, Antionette Payne, Walt Kirby, Debbie Ogilvie, Alan Hensley, Pam Jeffries, Barbara Donlon, Cathy Bennett, Matt Mesaros, Kristine Kline, Deborah Wilson, Eric Weiss, Julie Morel, Julie Hilderbrand, and Richard Rowe.

BRIEF CONTENTS

CONTENTS

lesson nine

COMMUNICATION AND DIVERSITY

IMPROVING COMMUNICATION, CELEBRATING DIVERSITY, AND MANAGING CONFLICTS 119

lesson ten

INFORMATION LITERACY

DETERMINING THE CREDIBILITY OF IDEAS AND RESOURCES 131

lesson eleven

LIVE

DEALING WITH STRESS IN POSITIVE WAYS 143

lesson twelve

PLAN

CREATING A DYNAMIC EMPLOYMENT PACKAGE AND JOB SEARCH PLAN 155

PREFACE

Cornerstones for College Success Compact is different from any other text.

Why?

Digital is here.

Students and instructors are engaging in more active learning and teaching. This requires a different kind of book. *Cornerstones for College Success Compact* is developed specifically for hybrid and online environments, and addresses the needs and challenges of students as digital learners. It aligns with learning outcomes from both the Student Success Course-Connect online course and MyStudentSuccessLab, making it ideal as a print companion paired with one of these technologies for hybrid or online learning.

Organized by learning outcome, both Student Success CourseConnect and MyStudentSuccessLab promote student engagement and help students "Start strong, Finish stronger" by building skills for ongoing personal and professional development. Student Success CourseConnect (www.pearsonlearningsolutions.com/courseconnect) is one of many award-winning CourseConnect online courses designed by subject matter experts and credentialed instructional designers that support a sequence of lessons, rich in content. MyStudentSuccessLab (www.mystudentsuccesslab.com) is an online solution with modules to support measurement using robust assessment with reporting capability, gradable activities, and professionalism topics.

Get only what you need.

When students are taking (or instructors are teaching) 1-credit-hour student success courses, it can be challenging to get through it all in the time available—and do so in an applied manner. There are a lot of "essentials' versions of books, but none offer the required application piece—until now.

Cornerstones for College Success Compact offers hallmark coverage of Bloom's taxonomy, SQ3R integration, information and financial literacy, and more. It is designed to provide an instructional foundation that addresses the "why" of learning. When paired with Student Success CourseConnect or MyStudentSuccessLab as an online companion, it actively augments learning with activities, assessments, and extended thought-provoking exercises students need to understand how to apply concepts.

BEGIN

THE GOAL OF CORNERSTONES FOR COLLEGE SUCCESS COMPACT AND OUR COMMITMENT TO YOU

Fotolia

"Talent alone won't make you a success. Neither will being in the right place at the right time, unless you are ready. The most important question is: 'Are you ready?'" —Johnny Carson

変化

If you look at the figure printed here you will see the Chinese symbol (verb) for "*to change*." It is made up of two symbols—the first means "*to transform*" or to be flexible. The second means "*to do or to deliver*." In its purest form, the symbol means to *deliver transformation*. That is what *Cornerstones for College Success Compact* is all about, helping you deliver or bring about transformation, positive change if you will, to your life. It is about helping you discover ways to change your thoughts, change your performance, and change your life.

Our goal in writing *Cornerstones* is to help you discover your academic, social, and personal strengths so that you can build on them and to provide *concrete and useful tools* that will help you make the changes necessary for your success. We believe that in helping you identify and transform areas that have challenged you in the past, you can *discover your true potential, learn more actively, and have the career you want and deserve.*

We know that your **time is valuable** and that you are pulled in countless directions with work, family, school, previous obligations, and many other tasks. For this reason, we have tried to provide only the most concrete, useful strategies and ideas to help you succeed in this class and beyond.

We have spent over 60 years collectively gathering the information, advice, suggestions, and activities on the following pages. This advice and these activities have come from trial and error, colleagues, former students, instructors across America, and solid research. We hope that you will enjoy them, learn from them, and, most of all, use them to change your life and move closer to your dreams.

Let the journey to positive change begin!

CORNERSTONES FOR COLLEGE SUCCESS COMPACT AND BLOOM'S TAXONOMY

Just What Is Bloom's Taxonomy Anyway?

Bloom's Taxonomy (also called Levels of Thinking and Learning) is simply a way of explaining the stages at which we all acquire information. These levels progress from simple learning and thinking (levels 1, 2, 3), to more complex learning and thinking (levels 4, 5, 6). In addition to having questions from Bloom's Taxonomy throughout your text, each lesson will end with an exercise called *Knowledge in Bloom*. This activity at the end of each lesson is included to help you process and apply the information from the lesson.

■ **LEVEL 1: Remember**

Simple recall of information

Words commonly associated with level 1 include: *write, list, define, describe, identify, tell, recognize, recite, match*

Example: *Define* critical thinking.

■ **LEVEL 2: Understand**

Understand / explain information

Words commonly associated with level 2 include: *summarize, paraphrase, interpret, discuss, explain, illustrate*

Example: Summarize the four steps in the critical thinking process.

■ LEVEL 3: Apply

Use the information

Words commonly associated with level 3 include: *apply, demonstrate, predict, solve, draw, calculate, modify, compute*

Example: Demonstrate the value of critical thinking to your success in college.

■ LEVEL 4: Analyze

Take apart the information for clarification—understand how parts work with one another

Words commonly associated with level 4 include: *test, infer, distinguish, compare/contrast*

Example: Outline the steps in the problem solving process.

■ LEVEL 5: Evaluate

Make personal judgments and justifications based on information

Words commonly associated with level 5 include: *decide, recommend, predict, judge, estimate, validate*

Example: Recommend three steps in making rational, creative decisions.

■ LEVEL 6: Create

Integrate your knowledge to produce new ideas and solutions

Words commonly associated with level 6 include: *compose, create, design, invent, propose, generate, write*

Example: Design a study plan that uses the four levels of critical thinking.

BLOOM'S TAXONOMY TRIANGLES

What Are All of Those Little Triangles?

Another feature that you will notice in your text is small triangles throughout followed by questions pertaining to the content. These triangles help you recognize which of the six levels of learning from Bloom's Taxonomy is being used. A quick reference chart of Bloom's Taxonomy (Revised) is on the inside front cover of this text.

SO, WHY USE BLOOM IN THE CORNERSTONES TEXT?

Bloom's Taxonomy is important to us all because it helps us determine the level at which we understand important information. For example, it is important to be able to answer questions at level 1, such as:

Abraham Lincoln was the _____ President of the United States.

Abraham Lincoln's wife's name was _____ _____ Lincoln.

However, it is also important to be able to answer questions at levels 5 and 6, such as:

Based on your knowledge of the Civil War era, predict what would have happened to the United States without the Emancipation Proclamation. Justify your answer.

Summarize the main events that led to President Lincoln's assassination.

As you can clearly see, there is a great difference between these levels of learning. The higher the level, the more information and knowledge you need to be able to understand to respond to the question or problem.

The end-of-lesson activity, ***Knowledge in Bloom,*** will help you process and demonstrate your knowledge at different levels. This is important because you will have instructors who ***teach and test*** at levels 1, 2, and 3, and those who ***teach and test*** at levels 5, 6, and 7. Learning to process and demonstrate your knowledge at every level can assist you in:

■ Doing well in other classes by providing a foundation for effective studying/learning

■ Learning to solve problems more thoroughly

■ Predicting exam questions

■ Learning how to critically evaluate and assess ideas and issues

■ Learning to thoroughly and objectively research topics for papers and presentations

■ Testing your own reading comprehension

A WORD ABOUT READING AND USING *CORNERSTONES*

We encourage you to read this text (and every text) with great care so that you can learn from the ideas presented within its pages. We also encourage you to **use** this book!

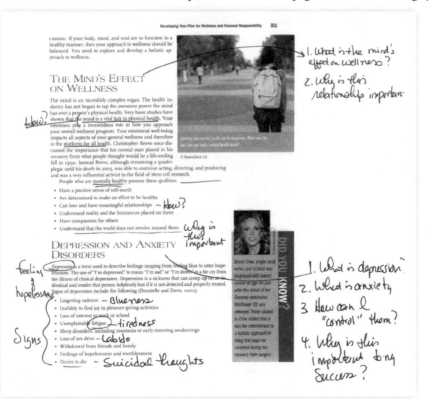

■ Write in the margins.

■ Circle important terms.

■ Highlight key phrases.

■ Jot down word definitions in the margins.

■ Dog-ear the pages.

■ Write questions that you have in the white spaces provided.

By treating this book as your "foundation to success," you will begin to see remarkable progress in your study practices, reading comprehension, and learning skills. Review this example of a marked page from another Cornerstones text.

lesson one
GROW

BUILDING A LIFE PLAN
THROUGH GOAL SETTING

Fotolia

"The greater danger for most of us is not that our aim is too high and we miss it, but that it is too low and we hit it."—Michangelo Buonarroti

GROW

Because you'll learn how to:

- Create long- and short-term goals that align with your personal mission statement

Because you'll be able to:

- Explain three cornerstones to academic success
- Analyze the relationship between change, values, motivation, and academic success
- Write a personal mission statement and long-term and short-term goals
- Analyze the characteristics of SMART goals

Knowledge in Bloom

Bloom's Taxonomy of Learning is a simple way of explaining the levels at which we all learn material and acquire information. The learning levels progress from basic to more complex learning and thinking. Examples are detailed below. Throughout this lesson, you'll see colorful triangles to the side of some activities. They let you know on which level of Bloom's Taxonomy the questions are based.

- **LEVEL 1: Remember**
  Define academic success.
- **LEVEL 2: Understand**
  Discuss the three major factors of academic success.
- **LEVEL 3: Apply**
  Demonstrate how your values affect your goal setting.
- **LEVEL 4: Analyze**
  Compare and contrast long- and short-term goals.
- **LEVEL 5: Evaluate**
  Predict how SMART goals will help your academic success.
- **LEVEL 6: Create**
  Write one major long-term goal.

MyStudentSuccessLab

MyStudentSuccessLab is an online solution designed to help you acquire and develop (or hone) the skills you need to succeed. You will have access to peer-led video presentations and develop core skills through interactive exercises and projects.

CREATING A ROAD MAP TO ACADEMIC SUCCESS

How Can Writing Goals Bring about Positive Change?

Our goal is to help you become the most successful student, thinker, citizen, leader, and lifelong learner that you can possibly be. This lesson is designed to help you understand some of the basic truths about college life and academic survival and to learn to set goals that help you attain academic and personal success. We believe that you can actually create your own academic success. So what is the formula for creating a successful future?

- Set clear, realistic goals that help you get better every day
- Recognize your abilities and build on them
- Recognize your weaknesses and strive to improve them
- Use your passion, motivation, and desire to make your goals and dreams a reality

Earning a college degree can open up new worlds for you. You will most likely make more money and enjoy a more challenging and rewarding career. Your chances of finding a good job and keeping that job are greatly increased. High school graduates have a much higher unemployment rate than college graduates. College should make you a better thinker who is more creative and open to a more diverse population. Study the chart in Figure 1.1 to understand how important a college degree is to you.

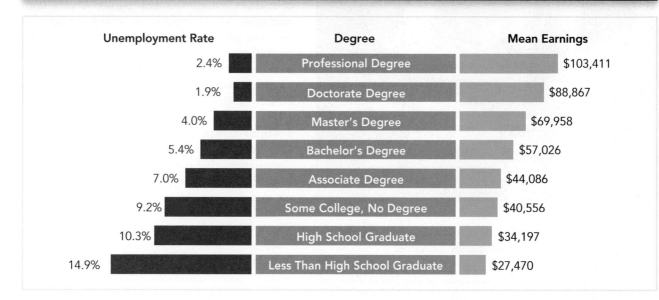

Figure 1.1 Education, Pay, and Unemployment Statistics of Full-Time Workers 25 and Over

Unemployment Rate	Degree	Mean Earnings
2.4%	Professional Degree	$103,411
1.9%	Doctorate Degree	$88,867
4.0%	Master's Degree	$69,958
5.4%	Bachelor's Degree	$57,026
7.0%	Associate Degree	$44,086
9.2%	Some College, No Degree	$40,556
10.3%	High School Graduate	$34,197
14.9%	Less Than High School Graduate	$27,470

Source: U.S. Bureau of the Census/U.S. Department of Labor (2011)

Earning a degree requires certain skills, academic abilities, dedication, hard work, goals, and focus. Going to college can be compared to taking a long road trip or setting out on a long journey to a desired destination, and it requires using a trusted road map to avoid unnecessary delays and detours. Millions of people have taken this journey and have been successful because they did what they needed to do—they did the right things at the right time, and they did them right.

Dropping out of college, however, is an equally common event. According to Rzadkiewicz (2011), "Approximately 35 percent of students who enter college will drop out during the first year." Some students leave because they made serious mistakes, such as partying too much and not going to class so they flunked out. Some couldn't manage their time; others couldn't manage their money. Still others didn't like their instructors and couldn't adjust to heavy workloads and the demanding rigor that college brings. Another group fails to complete the journey because they simply couldn't figure out how the system works so they gave up in frustration, anger, fear, and disappointment. This does not have to be you! You can complete this journey.

ADJUSTING TO THE CULTURE OF COLLEGE

What Are the Steps to Success?

College is not like high school! The work is faster paced; the expectations are much higher; you have to use higher level thinking skills and move beyond rote memorization; projects will require creativity and teamwork; you will have more freedom that you must manage wisely; assignments will demand that you research and discover resources; more technology will be incorporated; the instructors are not like your high school teachers; the student population is more diverse—the list of differences goes on and on! That's why going to college is so exciting! This is a once-in-a-lifetime experience to study, learn, grow, change, and move way down the road toward becoming the person you are meant to be.

There are many resources and people to help you—but you have to go to them. They will not seek you out. Research shows that only a small percentage of students actually seek help outside of class from instructors. Most instructors are willing to meet with you and give you assistance and advice, so when you feel lost or scared, get an appointment with the instructor in whose class you are struggling.

Most colleges and universities have numerous centers designed to provide additional help. You might find an academic center, a math/statistics lab, a writing center, a technology center, a language lab, and many others. You will find many student organizations that can be helpful to you. Ask your instructors and advisors for advice on where to go to get special assistance.

What is the most surprising thing you have learned about your institution's curriculum and policies thus far?
Fotolia

List three resources on your institution's campus that could help you improve and become more academically successful:

1. _____

_____

2. _____

_____

3. _____

_____

Level 1 Remember

THREE MAJOR FACTORS OF ACADEMIC SUCCESS

Why Are They So Important?

There are a number of factors that affect academic success: going to class, studying, avoiding cramming, taking good notes, hanging out with people who are serious about getting an education, not working too many hours in a part-time or full-time job, finding a tutor if you feel like you are falling behind—the list goes on and on, and they are all important factors. There are three factors, however, that make a major difference in whether you succeed or become part of the almost 40 percent of students who drop out.

The first factor is simply to understand completely why you came to college:

- Did you come because your parents expected you to?
- Did you come because you always knew you would go to college?
- Did you come because you couldn't find a decent job without an education?
- Did you come because your boyfriend, girlfriend, or partner was coming?
- Did you come because you truly love going to school?
- Did you come because you want to make more money and this is the ticket?
- Did you come because all your friends were going to college and you did not want to be left behind?
- Did you come because a college degree is a status symbol that you think you should have?

All of these points are valid reasons for deciding to go to college. But that is just the first step. Now that you are here and enrolled, you have to take steps beyond just getting in the front door. Now what? Do you know what you want to study? Do you have any idea if there are good jobs in the field you have chosen?

The second important factor is to take personal responsibility for your success. You may have looked forward to making your own decisions for a long time—now's your chance. Your mother won't be there to wake you up on time and make you go to class; most of your instructors won't track you down and tell you they are worried about you; your friends are worried about making it themselves so they won't be looking over your shoulder. You are on your own! You are going to experience a big culture shock if you are entering college directly from high school. If you are coming back to college after having been away for awhile, the technology factor may impact you hard. Regardless of the obstacles you might

What exactly is it going to take to achieve your biggest, most important goals?
Monkey Business Images/Shutterstock

encounter, you own them. It is up to you to do what it takes to succeed, so take ownership and responsibility!

The third major factor related to your academic success is to make connections with other people. Most people are social animals, at least to an extent. There are very few true loners who want to go off into the woods and live like a hermit. Most of us need a network of people in order to be healthy and happy. We need a strong support system when we go through difficult times; we need people with whom we can have fun and enjoy life; we need professional friends with whom we can collaborate and forge successful ideas; and we need instructors and advisors with whom we can discuss problems and concerns. This is a great time to build your network, whether it is social or professional. This is a great time to connect with people and to hone your communications skills.

> "I know the price of success: dedication, hard work, and constant devotion to the things you want to see happen."
> —Frank Lloyd Wright

THE TEN ESSENTIAL CORNERSTONES FOR SUCCESS IN A CHANGING WORLD

What Skills Are Needed to Be Successful?

If you are going to become the person you are capable of being, you will have to embrace change. Change, that you direct, creates opportunities for you to grow and prosper in ways you may have never imagined. You need to know this about change: It is a developed skill that takes

---

Figure 1.2 **Ten Essential Cornerstones for Success in a Changing World**

PASSION The ability to show a passion about one's mission and a willingness to align personal goals with education, talents, experiences, and skills. An ability to demonstrate concern not only about personal success, but also about the world and one's surroundings—a commitment to **civic literacy** and seeing oneself as "a citizen of the world."

MOTIVATION The ability to find the **inner strength and personal drive** to get up each day and face the world with an "I can, I will" attitude. The ability to develop a strong personal value and belief system that motivates you when the going gets tough. The ability to know who you are and never let anyone steal your identity or erode your personal ethics.

KNOWLEDGE The ability to **become highly skilled in a profession** or craft that will enable you to make a good living for yourself and your family in a rapidly changing workplace and to use lifelong learning to maintain your marketable skill sets. The ability to master important academic information beyond your major field in areas such as math, science, psychology, history, technology, economics, and communication and to practically apply that information in an evolving and highly technical work environment.

RESOURCEFULNESS The ability to apply **information literacy**—to know *where* to find information and the resources that will help you be successful in your academic studies and your chosen profession, and **how** to evaluate that information to determine if it is useful and accurate. The ability to look for and to seek new opportunities, options, and outcomes. The ability to imagine, integrate, and implement new ways of solving old problems.

CREATIVITY The ability to use **creativity and innovation** in solving problems that will enable you to anticipate new and emerging issues, to communicate and use what you know and what you have learned and discovered to

time, usually requires an attitude adjustment, and demands that you take action that moves you toward a goal. Change embraces two actions: letting go and holding on. Change requires letting go of bad habits, people who drag you down, and habits that are non-productive, and holding on to the positive people, strengths, and talents that have served you well in the past.

Whether we like it or not, a massive transformation is taking place all over the world. This change is making success more difficult today than it was in the past. Your college education should make you more competitive, give you an edge, and allow you to successfully build a good life for you and your family. **The Ten Essential Cornerstones for Success in a Changing World** (Figure 1.2) includes skills you will need for your success, personal independence, and continued growth in the new world that is emerging.

THE RELATIONSHIP BETWEEN CHANGE, VALUES, MOTIVATION, AND ACADEMIC SUCCESS

Why Are These Relationships Important to Success?

There is a definite relationship between being able to change, establishing a set of worthy values, becoming a motivated person, and achieving academic success; they are all mixed up together. We have already discussed the all-important ability of being able to change and move toward an expanded world filled with opportunities. Now, you need to get in touch with your value system and decide which values you need to hold onto and which ones need to be adjusted and added. Your values influence your choices and your choices influence your actions. We all make decisions and choices based on what we value. Values are simply those qualities, standards, and

answer critical questions and solve complex and demanding problems.

ADAPTABILITY   The ability to make good choices based on future opportunities and a changing workplace and to constantly **reinvent yourself** as change brings about necessity and opportunity. The ability to work effectively in a climate of changing priorities and uncertainty.

OPENMINDEDNESS   The ability to **accept and appreciate a highly diverse workplace** and the inherent differences and cultures that will be commonplace. The ability to listen to others with whom you disagree or with whom you may have little in common and learn from them and their experiences. The ability to learn a new language, even if your mastery is only at a primitive, broken, conversational level. The ability to conduct yourself in a respectable and professional manner.

COMMUNICATION   The ability to develop and maintain healthy, **supportive personal and professional**

relationships and to build a solid network of well-connected professionals who can help you and whom *you* can help in return.

ACCOUNTABILITY   The ability to **accept responsibility and be accountable** for all aspects of your future including your psychological well-being, your spiritual well-being, your relationships, your health, your finances, and your overall survival skills. Basically, you must develop a plan for the future that states, "If this fails, I'll do this," or "If this job is phased out, I'll do this," or "If this resource is gone, I'll use this," or "If this person won't help me, this one will."

VISION   The ability to guide your career path in a new global economy and to understand and take advantage of the inherent impact of worldwide competition—even if you live in a small town and work for a small "mom and pop" company. The ability to **"see" what is coming** and prepare for the changes, adapt to circumstances, and grow with grace and style.

beliefs that we consider to have merit or worth. Your values tend to guide your life and determine your choices. If you value attention, you will dress a certain way, or drive a flashy car, or do things that make people look at what you are doing. If you value an education, you will choose to study, to get assistance, and to turn in assignments on time. Someone who values a fit body will most likely choose to exercise, eat properly, and rest sufficiently. Below you will find a list of items. Read them carefully and circle the ones you truly value. If you value something that is not on the list, add it in the spaces at the bottom:

Honesty	Affection	Punctuality	Respect
Frankness	Open-Mindeness	Reliability	Trustworthiness
Sincerity	Wit/Humor	Spontaneity	Devotion
Frugality	Justice	Creativity	Caring
Spirituality	Friendliness	Energy	Intellect
Attentiveness	Conversational	Money	Security
Fine Dining	Beauty	Devotion	Enthusiasm
Positivism	Commitment	Foresightedness	Creativity
Organization	Learning	Listening	Giving
Control	Comfort	Knowledge	Courage
Athletic	Ability	Thoughtfulness	Independence
Safety	Fun	Excitement	Partying
Love	Friendship	Writing	Speaking
Reading	Family	Dependability	Teamwork
Time Alone	Time w/ Friends	Phone Calls	Walks
Exercise	Problem Solving	Empowerment	Integrity
Service to Others	Modesty	Strength	Tolerance
Imagination	Self-Esteem	Food	Power
Winning	Goals	Risk Taking	Change
Self Improvement	Forgiveness	Fairness	Optimism
Successful Career	Motivation	Trust	Direction in Life
Working	Hobbies	Books	Mentoring
Stability	_____	_____	_____

Now that you have circled or written what you value, choose the five that you value the most. In other words, if you were only allowed to value five things in life, what five would you list below? In the space to the right of each value, rank it from 1 to 5 (1 being the most important to you, your life, your relationships, your actions, your education, and your career).

Take your time and give serious consideration to this activity, as you will need to refer to this exercise later in this lesson.

List   **Rank**

_____   _____

_____   _____

_____   _____

_____   _____

Now, look at your #1. Where did this value originate?

_____

_____

Defend why this is the one thing you value more in life than anything else.

_____

_____

How does this one value motivate you?

_____

_____

Now that you are in touch with your personal values, you are ready to focus on developing a mission statement and on setting goals.

DEVELOPING YOUR PERSONAL MISSION STATEMENT

Why Is It Important to Have a Mission?

Many expert life coaches believe that creating a powerful personal mission statement is one of the best ways to change your life. It is important to get it right because your goals and plans for the future will emanate from this mission statement. Using a personal mission statement is the practice of living your life with direction and purpose rather than wandering like an explorer without a compass.

Your personal mission statement should be focused on these five things:

1. What is the purpose of my life?
2. What are my core strengths?
3. What do I value, believe in, and stand for?
4. What do I enjoy? What things lift me up and make me happy and fulfilled?
5. What action plan do I need to put in place to complement my purpose in life?

Important components of mission statements answer the following three questions: **What do I want to be, what do I want to do, and what do I want to have?**

Someone who seeks a career in owning a fine-dining restaurant, for example, might answer these questions in the following manner:

I would like to be a fine-dining restaurant owner, an owner of my own catering business, a wife and mother, a good daughter to my parents, a good sibling to my brother and sister, and a good community servant to people who need help.

I would like to do exciting things with my life like travel to all the continents and visit all the major cities in this country. I would like to take my family and parents to Broadway plays and scenic vacations. I would like to sponsor homeless children for camps.

I would like to have my own restaurant and later add three more restaurants of different types. I would like to have my own catering business that will support my charitable efforts. I would like to have a nice home for my family on 10 acres of land with horses and a pond.

Now, you should answer the following questions on the next page carefully and truthfully. You should please yourself—not someone else.

What do I want to *be?*

_____

_____

What do I want to *do?*

_____

_____

What do I want to *have?*

_____

_____

When writing your **personal mission statement,** you should begin with the end in mind. Look way down the road and imagine you have come to the end of your life. What will you want to have accomplished? In whose life will you hope you made a difference? What character and values do you want to be known for? Who do you want to be as a person, employee, spouse, parent, colleague, and friend? What do you dream of having and doing?

Now that you have determined what is really important to you, you are ready to begin writing your personal mission statement. This might take some time and you may want to continue to edit and adjust it for several days; you might even change this statement months from now. But get started *now*! Remember, no one can put boundaries on you except you. Don't worry about what anyone else will think about your ambitions and purpose. People around you have no idea how hard you are willing to work or how big your dreams are.

Having a personal mission statement is like having a compass with you at all times to guide your decisions. You are always pointed in the right direction, and you don't wander around lost.

A **sample mission statement** follows. As you can see, it is very specific about what this person is actually going to do:

I want to start my own business and own several restaurants and a catering business. My plan is to employ homeless people and people who have lost their jobs and give them a chance to own part of the business. When I have established four successful restaurants, I want to build a women's and children's shelter called Samantha's Place. I will use this shelter to teach women how to work in the restaurant and catering business and help them get jobs so they can take care of their children. I want to change lives, make a difference, and be an example to my own children. I want to marry my soul mate and live in the country in a nice home with our children. I want to travel to all the continents with my husband and children, and I want to retire financially secure.

Some other examples of personal mission statements using values follow:

I want to use my love of physical fitness to start a family-oriented gym with programs for people of all ages. I want to live a clean, healthy life and raise a family with children who are proud of me and who I am as a person. My goal is to help other people learn to eat healthy foods and exercise frequently. I would like to take my programs into schools and I hope to make videotapes to sell that will help me help others.

What sacrifices do you think you'll need to make in your personal and academic life to achieve your goals?
Pearson Education, Inc.

I want to start a plumbing company and own the largest company in Oklahoma City. I want to be able to take my family on international trips and provide them with a good living. I want to buy my mother a nice home and make her life comfortable. I would like to provide scholarships for deserving children who have grown up on Native American reservations to honor my grandmother who was Native American.

None of these may relate to you—and they don't have to. This is *your* mission statement, so make it belong to you; make it appealing and exciting enough that you want to spend your life working toward accomplishing it.

Now write your personal mission statement using the values you listed previously and your **be, do,** and **have** statements. Remember, you can erase and change and edit as much as you want to—just make it yours! You can start on this today and EDIT it next month. The important thing, however, is to think about it every day until you get it right for you.

Do you have a guiding statement for your life?
Tischenko Irina/ Shutterstock

Level 6 Create

My Personal Mission Statement:

_____

_____

_____

_____

_____

_____

USING YOUR LIFE'S MISSION TO SET LONG-TERM AND SHORT-TERM GOALS

Are Goals Really That Important?

When you have defined your mission, you are ready to set long- and short-term goals, the building blocks and foundation to a well-lived life. **Setting concrete goals is one of the best things you can do to attain your academic and professional accomplishments.** Few people take the time to sit down and think about where they are going with their one lifetime when it is a proven fact that a clear, well-defined, personal mission statement and written goals make a major difference in how much one accomplishes in life. Many people tend to drift around aimlessly with little purpose in what they do every day. They simply get up and do the same thing over and over again and wonder why their lives seem empty and meaningless and why they never seem to get ahead. Life is a series of choices, but many people just make decisions without thinking about the ramifications to their lives and the lives of their families. *Choose! Choose intentionally! We want you to make conscious choices about what you are doing and where you are going.*

> "A goal properly set is halfway reached."
> —Abraham Lincoln

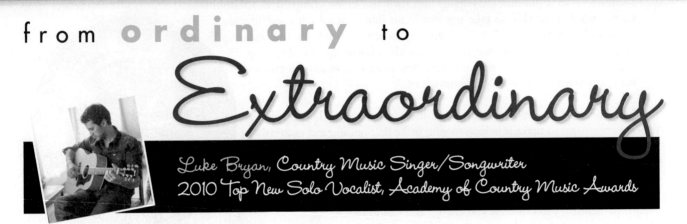

from **ordinary** to

Extraordinary

Luke Bryan, Country Music Singer/Songwriter
2010 Top New Solo Vocalist, Academy of Country Music Awards

Luke Bryan is the consummate goal setter. From the time he got his first guitar from his parents at age 14, he knew what he wanted to be: a country singer and performer. He set out to reach his goal by doing something every day to get better—one step at a time. Luke had talent, but he also had determination and a vision for what he could become. After playing in local clubs and working with local bands for several years while he finished high school, Luke was ready to make his move to the big time; he was heading for Nashville! But fate intervened in a devastating and untimely way. His brother, Chris, died in an automobile accident the same day he was to leave. Rather than go to Nashville, Luke went to college and paid his way through school performing with local bands.

After graduation, Luke went back home to South Georgia and began working with his father in farm-related businesses, but his heart was not in it. Finally, his father told him he had to go chase his dreams, so he left for Nashville. Within two months, Luke had landed a deal as a songwriter.

PHOTO: Kerri Edwards, Red Light Management

> *One of the biggest days of my life was signing a contract with Capitol Records. All my wishes and dreams came together right there in that room.*

Luke said, "One of the biggest days of my life was signing a contract with Capitol Records. All my wishes and dreams came together right there in that room." While performing locally, Luke was discovered by a Capitol Records representative. In 2007, his song *All My Friends Say* was climbing the charts at the same time that his song *Good Directions*, performed by another artist, was also headed up the charts. Luke was on his way toward reaching his goal! Today Luke Bryan is a bona fide country star, performing all over the country, traveling in his own tour bus, and living his dream.

EXTRAORDINARY REFLECTION

Luke was encouraged to go after his dreams by his family and friends. He believes that it is important to surround yourself with people who are on the move and believe in their dreams. How have your family and friends helped you reach your goals thus far?

> *"Happiness is not in the mere possession of money; it lies in the joy of achievement, in the thrill of creative effort."*
> *—Franklin D. Roosevelt*

CHARACTERISTICS OF SMART GOALS

After you have identified and solidified your long-term goals, you are ready to think about short-term goals that are really action plans that you do every day en route to your lifetime achievements. Before you do that, let's focus on writing SMART goals. SMART is a mnemonic that has been around for quite some time and has been used by many organizations

Figure 1.3   Smart Goals

SPECIFIC AND SIGNIFICANT—SMART goals are those that are detail oriented and will make a significant difference in your life if you achieve them.

MEASURABLE—You might hear this said at work: "What gets measured, gets done." You have to have a plan of how well you are going to do something or how much you are going to accomplish.

ACTION-ORIENTED AND ATTAINABLE—You have to do something to make goals happen, so action is required. These actions have to be under your control.

REALISTIC AND RELEVANT—Goals need to be realistically achievable so you don't get frustrated and quit. They need to be just out of reach so you have to stretch and grow to attain them.

TIME-BOUND OR DEADLINE ORIENTED/TRACKABLE—Goals need to be guided by a sense of urgency—you don't have forever to make something happen, so give yourself a realistic deadline for reaching your goals.

and individuals. Each letter in SMART indicates one criterion of a well-written goal. You can probably locate several versions of this plan, but for our purposes, we are going to define SMART as shown in Figure 1.3.

Using the SMART goals criteria, write one goal related to your personal academic achievement that you can accomplish this semester.

"Decide you want it more than you're afraid of it."
—Bill Cosby

_____

_____

_____

WRITING LONG-TERM AND SHORT-TERM GOALS

How Can Goal Setting Bring About Success?

In the beginning, you should write only a few goals that are important to you. Fewer goals will enable you to experience success that will be motivating to you. As you grow and learn, you will alter your goals and increase your list to fit your current circumstances. **Long-term goals** are exactly what they appear to be—they take time to accomplish. Long-term goals may take one year, five years, or even twenty years. Because they do take a long time, we tend to get discouraged, so we need to set **short-term goals** that are like intermediate steps en route to the bigger goals. Some people refer to short-term goals as enabling goals—they enable you to take the steps that help you reach your long-term plans. Short-term goals are based on your long-term goals and should be the steps that lead you to accomplishing the long-term goals. Both your short-term and long-term goals should relate to your personal mission statement.

REFLECTIONS on Goal Setting

If you study the lives and successes of most people who have "made it," you'll discover that they have some things in common: hard work, dedication, knowledge, and determination. However, the biggest commonality is the ability to set and work toward a goal. From Bill Gates to Michael Jordan to Barack Obama to Oprah, they decided what they wanted, developed a road map to achieve it, worked hard, and never gave up. Yes, they faced troubles and hard times, but they understood that giving up would only lead to failure. This is true of everyone. Set realistic goals, but also don't limit yourself by your current conditions. Through goal setting and hard work, you can have the things you want in this life.

Knowledge in Bloom

WRITING GOALS

Each lesson-end assessment is based on Bloom's Taxonomy of Learning. See the first page of this lesson for a quick review.

This activity uses levels 1–6 of the taxonomy

Using the My Personal Goal sheet that follows, write one short-term goal that is specific, relates to your mission statement, has action steps, has a narrative statement, has an "I deserve statement," and has a deadline. You can use this form as many times as you want to write separate goals.

My Personal Goal

To help you get started, use this goal-setting sheet as a template for this and future goals.

Name _____

Goal Statement (with action verb and target date)

_____

_____

Action Steps (concrete things you plan to do to reach your goal)

1. _____

   _____

   _____

   _____

2. _____

   _____

   _____

   _____

3. _____

   _____

   _____

   _____

Narrative Statement (how your life will look when you reach your goal)

_____

_____

_____

I deserve this goal because:

1. _____

   _____

   _____

2. _____

   _____

   _____

I hereby make this commitment to myself.

My Signature_____ Date _____

REFERENCE

Rzadkiewicz, C. C. (2011). Percentage of first year college drop out rates. Bright Hub. Retrieved January 20, 2012, from www.brighthub.com/education/college/articles/82378.aspx.

PRIORITIZE

CREATING AN ACADEMIC PRIORITY MANAGEMENT PLAN

Shutterstock

"Nothing is a waste of time if you use the experience wisely." —Rodin

Why read this lesson?

Because you'll learn how to:

- Create an academic priority management plan

Because you'll be able to:

- Identify effective priority management strategies
- Explain the importance of prioritizing activities
- Explain the advantages and disadvantages of various priority management tools
- Recommend strategies for avoiding priority management pitfalls
- Identify strategies to simplify your life

Knowledge in Bloom

Bloom's Taxonomy of Learning is a simple way of explaining the levels at which we all learn material and acquire information. The learning levels progress from basic to more complex learning and thinking. Examples are detailed below. Throughout this lesson, you'll see colorful triangles to the side of some activities. They let you know on which level of Bloom's Taxonomy the questions are based.

- **LEVEL 1: Remember**
  List three effective priority management strategies.
- **LEVEL 2: Understand**
  Explain the role self-discipline plays in managing your priorities.
- **LEVEL 3: Apply**
  Apply strategies for beginning your day with peace.
- **LEVEL 4: Analyze**
  Distinguish between work, school, and personal priority management tips.
- **LEVEL 5: Evaluate**
  Evaluate your ability to set priorities.
- **LEVEL 6: Create**
  Create a personal priority management plan.

MyStudentSuccessLab

MyStudentSuccessLab is an online solution designed to help you acquire and develop (or hone) the skills you need to succeed. You will have access to peer-led video presentations and develop core skills through interactive exercises and projects.

EFFECTIVE PRIORITY MANAGEMENT STRATEGIES

Why Is Taking Control Important?

You can definitely say four things about time: *It is fair. It does not discriminate. It treats everyone the same. Everyone has all there is.* No person has any more or less hours in a day than the next person. In a 24-hour span we all have 1440 minutes. No more. No less. There is one more thing you can definitely say about time: *it can be cruel and unrelenting.* Time is one of the few things in our lives that we cannot stop. There are no time-out periods, no breaks, and try as we might, we can't turn it back, shut it down, or stop it. The good news, however, is that by learning how to manage our time more effectively, we don't need to slow it down or stop it.

Before we examine some effective priority management strategies, take a moment and complete the Priority Management Assessment in Figure 2.1. Be honest and truthful with your responses. Be sure to read and pay close attention to each statement because each one is an effective priority management strategy. The results of your score are located after the assessment.

PRIORITY MANAGEMENT AND SELF-DISCIPLINE

What Does It Take to Finish the Job?

> "Self-discipline is teaching ourselves to do the things necessary to reach our goals without becoming sidetracked by bad habits."
>
> —Denis Waitley

Priority management is actually about managing you! It is about taking control and assuming responsibility for the time you are given on this Earth. The sooner you understand and get control of how you use your time, the quicker you will be on your way to becoming successful in school, in your career, and in many other activities. Learning to manage your time is a lesson that you will use in all aspects of your life. Actually, *you can't control time,* but you can control yourself. Priority management is basically self-discipline—and self-discipline involves self-motivation. Time management is paying attention to how you are spending your most valuable resource and then devising a plan to use it more effectively.

The word *discipline* comes from the Latin word meaning "to teach." Therefore, *self-discipline* is really about "teaching ourselves" (Waitley, 1997). Self-discipline implies that you have the ability to teach yourself how to get more done when things are going well and when they are not going so well. If you have self-discipline, you have learned how to hold it all together when things get tough, when you feel beaten, and when defeat seems just around the corner. It also means that when you have important tasks to complete, you can temporarily pull yourself

Figure 2.1   Priority Management Assessment

Answer the questions below with the following scale:

1 = Not at all   2 = Rarely   3 = Sometimes   4 = Often   5 = Very often

1.	I prioritize my tasks every day and work from my priority list.	1 2 3 4 5
2.	I work hard to complete tasks on time and not put them off until the last minute.	1 2 3 4 5
3.	I take time to plan and schedule the next day's activities the night before.	1 2 3 4 5
4.	I have made time during my daily schedule to study and get my projects completed so that I can have more quality time at home.	1 2 3 4 5
5.	I study and get my work done before I take fun breaks.	1 2 3 4 5
6.	I analyze my assignments to determine which ones are going to take the most time and then work on them first and most often.	1 2 3 4 5
7.	I have analyzed my daily activities and determined where I actually spend my time.	1 2 3 4 5
8.	I know how to say "no" and do so frequently.	1 2 3 4 5
9.	I know how to avoid distractions and how to work through unexpected interruptions.	1 2 3 4 5
10.	I do not let "fear of the unknown" keep me from working on a project.	1 2 3 4 5
11.	I know how to overcome apathy and boredom toward a project.	1 2 3 4 5
12.	I know how to fight and overcome my own laziness.	1 2 3 4 5
13.	I know how to reframe a project that may not interest me so that I can see the benefits from it and learn from it.	1 2 3 4 5
14.	I know how to break down a major, complex, or overwhelming task to get it done in pieces and then put it all together.	1 2 3 4 5
15.	I build time into my schedule on a daily or weekly basis to deal with "unexpected" interruptions or distractions.	1 2 3 4 5

YOUR TOTAL SCORE: _____

RESULTS: **60–75**   You manage your priorities well and you know how to build a schedule to get things done. Your productivity is high. You don't let procrastination rule your life.

45–59   You are good at doing some things on time, but you tend to procrastinate too much. Learning how to build and work from a priority list may help you manage your time more effectively.

30–44   You need to work hard to change your priority management skills and learn how to set realistic goals. Procrastination is probably a major issue for you, causing you much stress and worry. Working from a priority list can help you greatly.

29 or below   Your priority management skills are very weak and without change and improvement, your success plan could be in jeopardy. You could benefit from learning to set realistic goals, working from a priority list, and reframing your thought process toward tasks.

away from enjoyable situations and fun times until those tasks are completed. Consider the chart in Figure 2.2 regarding self-discipline. Self-discipline is really about four things: Making Choices, Making Changes, Using Willpower, and Taking Responsibility.

Figure 2.3 lists ten important ways to simplify your life. Using Figure 2.4, compile a list that can help you simplify your life in each category. Add **only** those things to the list that you can actually **do** on a daily basis.

Figure 2.2   Components of Self-Discipline

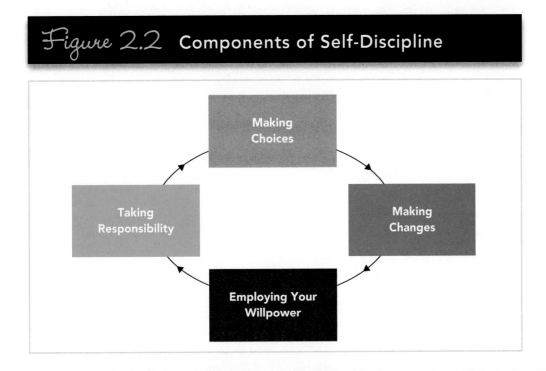

Figure 2.3   10 Important Ways to Simplify Your Life

By using these few simple strategies, you can begin to simplify your life and become much more effective:

1. Know what you value and work hard to eliminate activities that are not in conjunction with your core value system. This can be whittled down to one statement: "Identify what is important to you. Eliminate everything else." Match your priorities with your goals and values.

2. Get away from technology for a few hours a day. Turn off your computer, cell phone, iPod, and other devices that can take time from what you value.

3. Learn to delegate to others. Children can learn to do tasks at home. Roommates need to do their share.

4. Make a list of everything you are doing. Prioritize this list into what you enjoy doing and what fits into your value system. If you can only feasibly do three or four of these activities per day, draw a line after number four and move the rest to the next day.

5. Do what is essential for the wellbeing of you and your family and eliminate everything else. Delegate some things to family members of all ages that they can accomplish.

6. Don't waste time saving money. This doesn't mean to not save money—it means not to be "pound wise and penny foolish." Spend money to save time. In other words, don't drive across town to save three cents per gallon on fuel or ten cents for a gallon of milk.

7. Clean your home of clutter and mess. De-clutter and organize. Make sure everything has a place. Do the same thing at work. Get rid of things you don't need at home and at work.

8. Donate everything you don't need or use to charity. Simplifying your life may also mean simplifying your closets, drawers, cabinets, and garage. Go through yours and eliminate everything that does not bring you joy or have sentimental value. If you don't love it, need it, or use it, let it go and move on.

9. Clean up the files on your computer. Erase everything that you don't need or want so that you can find material more easily.

10. Live in the moment. Although it is important to plan for the future, it is equally important to live today! Spend a few moments each morning and afternoon reflecting on all of the abundance in your life. Learn to give thanks and learn to do nothing. Count your blessings.

Source: Adapted from Babauta (2012) and Get More Done (2012).

Figure 2.4 **Ten Ways to Simplify Your Life**

Two things I can do to simplify my life at home	
Two things I can do to simplify my life at work	
Two things I can do to simplify my life at school	
Two things I can do to simplify my life with my children	
Two things I can do to simplify my life with my spouse/partner/loved one	
Two things I can do to simplify my economics (financial matters)	

"No" Is a Powerful Word—Use It!

- Think before you answer out loud with an insincere or untrue "Yes." Tell the person who is asking that you need time to think about it because you are already stretched pretty thin. Don't make an immediate decision.

- Review your schedule to see if you really have the time to do a quality job. ("If you have to have an answer immediately, it is 'No.' If you can wait a few days for me to finish project X, and review my schedule, I'll take a careful look at it.")

- Learn the difference between assertiveness (politely declining) and rudeness (have you lost your mind?).

- Say "No" at the right times (to the wrong things) so that you can say "Yes" at the appropriate times (to the right things).

- Learn how to put yourself and your future first (for a change). By doing this, you can say "Yes" more often later on.

- Inform others of your priority management schedule so that they will have a better understanding of why you say "No."

- If you must say "Yes" to an unwanted project (something at work, for example), try to negotiate a deadline that works for everyone—you first!

- Keep your "No" short. If you have to offer an explanation, be brief so that you don't talk yourself into doing something you can't do and to avoid giving false hope to the other person. If the answer is "No" right now and it will be "No" in the future, say "No" now and don't smile because that indicates "Maybe."

> *"Time is the most valuable and most perishable of our possessions."*
> —John Randolph

- If you feel you simply have to say yes, try to trade off with the other person and ask him or her to do something on your list.

- Put a time limit on your "Yes." For example, you might agree to help someone but you could say, "I can give you thirty minutes and then I have to leave."

MORE PRIORITY MANAGEMENT STRATEGIES

What Are the Tips for Managing School, Work, and Personal Time?

Good priority management often boils down to doing a few things extremely well and doing them over and over. Learning to organize your academic calendar can make a major difference in your college success. When you go to work, the big things count—but so do the little ones! If you have a family, you will need to be highly organized so you can spend quality time with them.

- Break up big jobs into little ones so they don't overwhelm you.
- Allow yourself enough time to complete a task with extra time in case there is a glitch. Work expands to fill up whatever amount of time you have so push yourself to complete the job in a reasonable time frame.
- Set up regular times to study and stick to them.
- When you have a major project, start early and work on it every day. Avoid having to cram for school or work projects.
- When working on a project, set reasonable goals that you can meet in 20–25 minute blocks.
- Take short breaks; get up from your computer and move around. Leave your desk for lunch and breaks. You'll come back refreshed.
- Allow yourself longer than you think you need for a project so you don't have to stay up all night.
- Don't get too involved with outside organizations and commitments that steal your time and make you look slack at school and at work.
- Start on the most difficult, boring jobs first. Reward yourself with something you enjoy after you have completed a good block of work.
- Weed out personal belongings; get rid of clutter that takes your time. Streamline your home, your workspace, and your home desk.
- File things as you go; don't pile them in stacks. Don't allow yourself to be one of those people who would rather "pile than file" because you will never be able to find important documents.
- If you have children, give each one a workspace with his/her own supplies. Give each child a file drawer or box to keep important papers that they will need again. You are teaching them priority management and organization skills.
- Handle paperwork immediately and only once.
- Organize your workspace and designate a specific place for your supplies. Keep supplies on hand so you don't run out at a crucial time.
- Prepare to be successful at work or school by getting ready the evening before. Decide what you are going to wear; iron your clothes if they need it; pack your supplies for the next day.
- Keep contact information in your phone, computer, iPod, or other system to track important phone numbers and addresses you use frequently.

Do you think saying no is rude or necessary?
Brian McEntire/ iStockphoto

- Plan a rotation schedule for housework. Clean one room each day.
- Organize your closets and dresser drawers, ridding yourself of clutter and things you don't use anymore.
- Fill up your gas tank the night before to avoid stress in the morning.
- If you are a perfectionist, get over it! Some things need to be perfect, but most don't.
- Take time to do things you love and create a healthy balance in your life. If you reward the completion of a big job by immediately beginning another big job, you have a good chance of becoming a workaholic.
- If you have children, schedule at least one hour a week with each one. Make this a happy, special time. Sunday nights are great for family night.
- Make meals happy. Sit down with family and/or friends at least three times a week. Allow each person to tell about his or her day.
- Put fun days on your calendar and keep them sacred.
- Put family and friend days on your calendar and ask for help to get things done so you can relax and enjoy time together.

THE IMPORTANCE OF PRIORITIZATION, PLANNING, AND PREPARING

What Is the Importance of These Three Strategies?

In the past, you may have said to yourself, *"I don't have time to plan." "I don't like to be fenced in and tied to a rigid schedule." "I have so many responsibilities that planning never works."* Scheduling does not have to be a tedious chore or something you dread. Scheduling can be your lifeline to more free time. After all, if **you** build your own schedule, it is yours! As much as you are able, build your schedule the way you want and need it.

To manage your time successfully, you need to spend some time planning. To plan successfully, you need a calendar that has a week-at-a-glance or month-at-a-glance section, as well as sections for daily notes and appointments. You can download a free calendar from the Internet, create one using Word or another computer program, or get a free calendar app.

PRIORITIZING AND PLANNING PERSONAL AND SCHOOL TASKS

Planning and Organizing for School

Each evening, you should take a few minutes (and literally, that is all it will take) and sit in a quiet place and make a list of all that needs to be done tomorrow. Successful time management comes from planning the **night before**! Let's say your list includes:

Research speech project	Exercise
Study for Finance test on Friday	Buy birthday card for mom
Read Chapter 13 for Chemistry	Wash the car

Meet with Chemistry study group
Attend English class at 8:00 am
Attend Mgmt. class at 10:00 am
Work from 2:00–6:00 pm

Take shirts to dry cleaner
Buy groceries
Call Janice about weekend

Now, you have created a list of tasks that you will face tomorrow. Next, separate this list into three categories:

Must Do	Need to Do	Would Like to Do
Read Chapter 13 for Chemistry	Research speech project	Wash the car
Study for Finance test on Friday	Buy birthday card for mom	Call Janice about weekend
Exercise	Take shirts to cleaner	
English class at 8:00 am	Buy groceries	
Mgmt. class at 10:00 am		
Meet with Chemistry study group		
Work from 2:00–6:00 pm		

Don't get too excited yet. Your time management plan is *not* finished. The most important part is still ahead of you. Now, you will need to rank the items in order of their importance. You will put a 1 by the most important tasks, a 2 by the next most important tasks, and so on, in each category.

Must Do	Need to Do	Would Like to Do
1 Read Chapter 13 for Chemistry	1 Research speech project	2 Wash the car
2 Study for Finance test on Friday	2 Buy birthday card for mom	1 Janice about weekend Call
3 Exercise	3 Take shirts to cleaner	
1 English class at 8:00 am	2 Buy groceries	
1 Mgmt. class at 10:00 am		
2 Meet with Chemistry study group		
1 Work from 2:00–6:00 pm		

Now, you have created a plan to actually get these tasks done! Not only have you created your list, but now you have divided them into important categories, ranked them, and you have made a written commitment to these tasks.

Now, take these tasks and schedule them into your daily calendar (see Figure 2.5). You would schedule category 1 first (Must Do), category 2 next (Need to Do), and category 3 (Would Like to Do) last. Remember, never keep more than one calendar. Always carry it with you and always schedule your tasks immediately so that you won't forget them. Consider using a scheduling app to help you.

Figure 2.5 Daily Calendar

DAY	Monday		
Time	**Task**	**Priority**	**Complete?**
6:00			Yes___ No
6:30			Yes___ No
7:00	Study for finance		Yes___ No
7:30	↓		Yes___ No
8:00	English 101		Yes___ No
8:30			Yes___ No
9:00	↓		Yes___ No
9:30	Read Pg. 1–10 of Chem. Chapter		Yes___ No
10:00	Management 210		Yes___ No
10:30			Yes___ No
11:00	↓		Yes___ No
11:30	Finish Reading Chem. Chapter		Yes___ No
12:00			Yes___ No
12:30	↓		Yes___ No
1:00	Meet w/Chemistry group (take lunch)		Yes___ No
1:30	↓		Yes___ No
2:00	Work		Yes___ No
2:30			Yes___ No
3:00			Yes___ No
3:30			Yes___ No
4:00			Yes___ No
4:30			Yes___ No
5:00			Yes___ No
5:30			Yes___ No
6:00	↓		Yes___ No
6:30	Dinner/run by grocery store		Yes___ No
7:00	↓		Yes___ No
7:30	Internet Research for speech		Yes___ No
8:00			Yes___ No
8:30	↓		Yes___ No
9:00	call Janice @ w/end		Yes___ No
9:30			Yes___ No

USING PRIORITY MANAGEMENT TOOLS EFFECTIVELY

Is Getting Control of Time and Life Really Possible?

There are several very valuable time management tools that can help you get a handle on how to manage your time. But remember—these tools only work if you work! Study the list below and decide which tools will be effective for you.

- **Purchase a paper planner/calendar** that allocates one to two pages per day. This will give you enough room to list your planned schedule and record notes, phone numbers, directions, and comments. Make yourself write everything in this planner; don't write an important phone number on the back of an envelope where you are likely to lose it.

from ordinary to Extraordinary

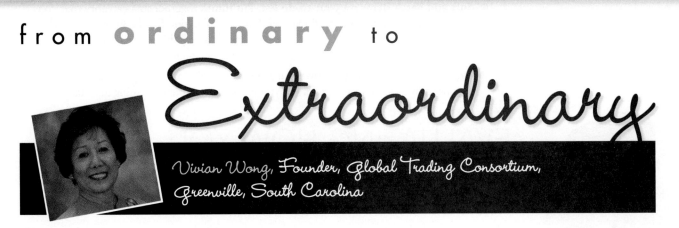

Vivian Wong, Founder, Global Trading Consortium, Greenville, South Carolina

Vivian Wong is an amazing woman who built a business empire by using her time wisely, setting priorities, thinking big, and working hard and smart. Born in China, Vivian and her husband started thinking about coming to America in the '60s. An American businessman gave them $100 and told them to acquire passports. It took them a year to get training visas, but with this task accomplished, they headed to South Carolina, leaving their little girl behind with grandparents. Because they were homesick, they returned home to China after ten months, but upon arriving there, they realized Greenville, South Carolina, was home, so they returned with their little girl. During the time that Vivian and her husband were learning how to succeed in their new country, they were blessed with twin girls, so now they had three children for whom they had to provide.

Not one to be satisfied with just getting by, Vivian and her husband set out to do better than "just put food on the table." Vivian stated, "We spent the first twenty years in America simply trying to earn a meager living and put food on the table." Her husband trained for restaurant ownership

> *We spent the first twenty years in America simply trying to earn a meager living and put food on the table.*

in Washington, D.C., and in 1970, they opened their first Chinese restaurant, followed by others in 1975, 1976, and 1988. Dreaming big, Vivian became interested in commercial real estate and began to branch out, acquiring hotels and other business interests. Today she and her brother have opened a hotel chain in China called Hotel Carolina, and are partners and franchisees of the Medicine Shoppe, China's first American pharmacy. Vivian and her husband own a large business park and foreign trade zone in South Carolina, and she is a partner in three banks. By working hard and smart, setting her priorities, and taking calculated risks, Vivian Wong succeeded beyond her wildest dreams. She moved from ordinary to extraordinary.

EXTRAORDINARY REFLECTION

Mrs. Wong mentions how important it is to work hard and smart, to set priorities, and to take calculated risks. How can these same strategies help you succeed in college and beyond?

If you are under stress or in a rush, you know exactly where your important information is—your planner/calendar. Get in the habit of looking a week and a month ahead on a daily basis to avoid having something important and time consuming slip up on you.

- An **electronic planner/calendar** is also a good tool if you have an electronic device that you always have with you. It can serve the same purpose as a paper calendar, so if you prefer it and can manage it, use it. Some electronic calendars will send you an e-mail reminder, which is helpful to some people.

- Making a **daily "to-do" list** and transferring it to your planner/calendar is a must! Put the item in the place on your calendar where you need to get it done. If it is July now and you don't need to have this done until September, put it in the September section so you don't forget.

- **Sort and batch items on your to-do list.** Put things together in a category that you might be able to do in a related manner. For example, look for the book you need in your Literature class when you are in the library researching articles for your term paper. Purge things that are not essential and not personally important to you.
- **Organize your desk and your living space.** Do yourself a favor and get organized, especially in your study area. Have a place for everything, and always put everything in its place.

EVALUATING HOW YOU SPEND YOUR TIME

Where Does the Time Go?

So how do you find out where your time goes? The same way that you find out where your money goes—you track it. Every 15 minutes for one week, you will record exactly how you spent that time. This exercise may seem a little tedious at first, but if you will complete the process over a period of a week, you will have a much better concept of where your time is being used. You will probably be surprised at where your time really goes.

Take your plan with you and keep track of your activities during the day. To make things simple, round off tasks to 15-minute intervals. For example, if you start walking to class at 7:08, you might want to mark off the time block that begins with 7:00. If you finish class and return to your home at 9:40, you can register 9:45 on your calendar. You will also want to note the activity so you can evaluate how you spent your time later. Study the example that is provided for you in Figure 2.6.

Have you ever allowed procrastination to stress you out? What was the result?
Fotolia

Figure 2.6 How Do You Really Spend Your Time?

7:00	get up	7:00					12:15
	& shower	7:15					12:30
	✗	7:30			Walked to Union		12:45
	Breakfast	7:45	1:00		Ate lunch		1:00
8:00		8:00					1:15
		8:15					1:30
	Read paper	8:30			Talked w/ Joe		1:45
	Walked to class	8:45	2:00				2:00
9:00	English 101	9:00			Went to book		2:15
		9:15			store		2:30
		9:30			Walked to		2:45
		9:45	3:00		my room		3:00
10:00		10:00			Called Ron		3:15
		10:15					3:30
		10:30					3:45
	Walked to class	10:45	4:00		Watched		4:00
11:00	History 210	11:00			TV		4:15
		11:15					4:30
		11:30			Walked to		4:45
		11:45	5:00		library		5:00
12:00		12:00					5:15

In Figure 2.7 you will find a daily time log for you to use for this exercise. Remember to take these pages with you and record how you are spending your time during the day. As you progress through the week, try to improve the use of your time. When you finish this exercise, review how you spent your time and plan strategies for using your time more wisely.

After you have kept your daily time logs for two days, analyze how you are spending your time and determine how you might spend it more wisely. Determine how and with whom you wasted time and identify ways you might improve your time management strategies.

Level 4 Analyze

AVOIDING PRIORITY MANAGEMENT PITFALLS

Is It Possible to Plan Your Life?

We have looked at numerous priority management tips to guide you in developing your own academic time management plan. Study the following list of the most common priority management pitfalls, the kinds of problems that keep students from succeeding in school:

- **Becoming overwhelmed with new-found freedom.** Many new college students simply don't know how to manage their time. They have always had teachers who kept reminding them or parents who checked up on them. You are truly on your own now, and you have to take control.

- **Failure to maintain a to-do list.** This is one of the simplest priority management tools you can use, yet one of the most effective. One of the last things you do every evening is to make a list of what you need to do the next day. Begin the day prepared to have a good day!

- **Failure to prioritize.** A list is not much good unless you have put priority numbers by each item. This is the downfall of many priority management plans—people fail to rank their entries. Select the things that are most important, have to be done soon, and will make the biggest difference for your academic success. But don't forget the small things as well. Don't use a system that overcomplicates the process and becomes a burden.

- **Procrastinating until it is too late to do a good job.** Many people are procrastinators; they never do their best work because they put things off until they have to rush or cram or simply not get the work done.

- **Having no definitive goals and plans.** Goals are like a road map. Not setting goals can be compared to a rudderless ship—you go around and around with no direction.

- **Saying "Yes" when you should have said "No."** If you are constantly taking on other people's priorities and ignoring your own, you need to learn to say "No."

- **Trying to be a perfectionist and spending too much time on a project.** Get over it! No one is perfect. Some things really do have to be perfect, but most can simply be done well before you move on.

- **Multi-tasking to the point that you get nothing of substance completed or you spend all your time working.** Some people try to do so much that they focus all their time on work. This is not healthy! You need to plan time for fun and joy, and you need to spend time with friends and family.

- **Failing to manage distractions.** There are so many ways to become distracted, and most of them are much more fun that doing academic work. When you have finished having fun, the work is still there, and now the stress sets in. This is a cardinal rule of priority management: Work first, then play.

"Don't wait. The time will never be just right."

—Napoleon Hill

Figure 2.7 **Daily Time Sheet**

	Monday			Tuesday			Wednesday	
6:00	6:00	6:00		6:00	6:00		6:00	
	6:15			6:15			6:15	
	6:30			6:30			6:30	
	6:45			6:45			6:45	
7:00	7:00	7:00		7:00	7:00		7:00	
	7:15			7:15			7:15	
	7:30			7:30			7:30	
	7:45			7:45			7:45	
8:00	8:00	8:00		8:00	8:00		8:00	
	8:15			8:15			8:15	
	8:30			8:30			8:30	
	8:45			8:45			8:45	
9:00	9:00	9:00		9:00	9:00		9:00	
	9:15			9:15			9:15	
	9:30			9:30			9:30	
	9:45			9:45			9:45	
10:00	10:00	10:00		10:00	10:00		10:00	
	10:15			10:15			10:15	
	10:30			10:30			10:30	
	10:45			10:45			10:45	
11:00	11:00	11:00		11:00	11:00		11:00	
	11:15			11:15			11:15	
	11:30			11:30			11:30	
	11:45			11:45			11:45	
12:00	12:00	12:00		12:00	12:00		12:00	
	12:15			12:15			12:15	
	12:30			12:30			12:30	
	12:45			12:45			12:45	
1:00	1:00	1:00		1:00	1:00		1:00	
	1:15			1:15			1:15	
	1:30			1:30			1:30	
	1:45			1:45			1:45	
2:00	2:00	2:00		2:00	2:00		2:00	
	2:15			2:15			2:15	
	2:30			2:30			2:30	
	2:45			2:45			2:45	
3:00	3:00	3:00		3:00	3:00		3:00	
	3:15			3:15			3:15	
	3:30			3:30			3:30	
	3:45			3:45			3:45	
4:00	4:00	4:00		4:00	4:00		4:00	
	4:15			4:15			4:15	
	4:30			4:30			4:30	
	4:45			4:45			4:45	
5:00	5:00	5:00		5:00	5:00		5:00	
	5:15			5:15			5:15	
	5:30			5:30			5:30	
	5:45			5:45			5:45	
6:00	6:00	6:00		6:00	6:00		6:00	
	6:15			6:15			6:15	
	6:30			6:30			6:30	
	6:45			6:45			6:45	
7:00	7:00	7:00		7:00	7:00		7:00	
	7:15			7:15			7:15	
	7:30			7:30			7:30	
	7:45			7:45			7:45	
8:00	8:00	8:00		8:00	8:00		8:00	
	8:15			8:15			8:15	
	8:30			8:30			8:30	
	8:45			8:45			8:45	
9:00	9:00	9:00		9:00	9:00		9:00	
	9:15			9:15			9:15	
	9:30			9:30			9:30	
	9:45			9:45			9:45	
10:00	10:00	10:00		10:00	10:00		10:00	
	10:15			10:15			10:15	
	10:30			10:30			10:30	
	10:45			10:45			10:45	
11:00	11:00	11:00		11:00	11:00		11:00	
	11:15			11:15			11:15	
	11:30			11:30			11:30	
	11:45			11:45			11:45	
12:00	12:00	12:00		12:00	12:00		12:00	

Thursday		Friday		Saturday		Sunday		
6:00	6:00	6:00	6:00	6:00	6:00	6:00	6:00	6:00
	6:15		6:15		6:15		6:15	6:15
	6:30		6:30		6:30		6:30	6:30
	6:45		6:45		6:45		6:45	6:45
7:00	7:00	7:00	7:00	7:00	7:00	7:00	7:00	7:00
	7:15		7:15		7:15		7:15	7:15
	7:30		7:30		7:30		7:30	7:30
	7:45		7:45		7:45		7:45	7:45
8:00	8:00	8:00	8:00	8:00	8:00	8:00	8:00	8:00
	8:15		8:15		8:15		8:15	8:15
	8:30		8:30		8:30		8:30	8:30
	8:45		8:45		8:45		8:45	8:45
9:00	9:00	9:00	9:00	9:00	9:00	9:00	9:00	9:00
	9:15		9:15		9:15		9:15	9:15
	9:30		9:30		9:30		9:30	9:30
	9:45		9:45		9:45		9:45	9:45
10:00	10:00	10:00	10:00	10:00	10:00	10:00	10:00	10:00
	10:15		10:15		10:15		10:15	10:15
	10:30		10:30		10:30		10:30	10:30
	10:45		10:45		10:45		10:45	10:45
11:00	11:00	11:00	11:00	11:00	11:00	11:00	11:00	11:00
	11:15		11:15		11:15		11:15	11:15
	11:30		11:30		11:30		11:30	11:30
	11:45		11:45		11:45		11:45	11:45
12:00	12:00	12:00	12:00	12:00	12:00	12:00	12:00	12:00
	12:15		12:15		12:15		12:15	12:15
	12:30		12:30		12:30		12:30	12:30
	12:45		12:45		12:45		12:45	12:45
1:00	1:00	1:00	1:00	1:00	1:00	1:00	1:00	1:00
	1:15		1:15		1:15		1:15	1:15
	1:30		1:30		1:30		1:30	1:30
	1:45		1:45		1:45		1:45	1:45
2:00	2:00	2:00	2:00	2:00	2:00	2:00	2:00	2:00
	2:15		2:15		2:15		2:15	2:15
	2:30		2:30		2:30		2:30	2:30
	2:45		2:45		2:45		2:45	2:45
3:00	3:00	3:00	3:00	3:00	3:00	3:00	3:00	3:00
	3:15		3:15		3:15		3:15	3:15
	3:30		3:30		3:30		3:30	3:30
	3:45		3:45		3:45		3:45	3:45
4:00	4:00	4:00	4:00	4:00	4:00	4:00	4:00	4:00
	4:15		4:15		4:15		4:15	4:15
	4:30		4:30		4:30		4:30	4:30
	4:45		4:45		4:45		4:45	4:45
5:00	5:00	5:00	5:00	5:00	5:00	5:00	5:00	5:00
	5:15		5:15		5:15		5:15	5:15
	5:30		5:30		5:30		5:30	5:30
	5:45		5:45		5:45		5:45	5:45
6:00	6:00	6:00	6:00	6:00	6:00	6:00	6:00	6:00
	6:15		6:15		6:15		6:15	6:15
	6:30		6:30		6:30		6:30	6:30
	6:45		6:45		6:45		6:45	6:45
7:00	7:00	7:00	7:00	7:00	7:00	7:00	7:00	7:00
	7:15		7:15		7:15		7:15	7:15
	7:30		7:30		7:30		7:30	7:30
	7:45		7:45		7:45		7:45	7:45
8:00	8:00	8:00	8:00	8:00	8:00	8:00	8:00	8:00
	8:15		8:15		8:15		8:15	8:15
	8:30		8:30		8:30		8:30	8:30
	8:45		8:45		8:45		8:45	8:45
9:00	9:00	9:00	9:00	9:00	9:00	9:00	9:00	9:00
	9:15		9:15		9:15		9:15	9:15
	9:30		9:30		9:30		9:30	9:30
	9:45		9:45		9:45		9:45	9:45
10:00	10:00	10:00	10:00	10:00	10:00	10:00	10:00	10:00
	10:15		10:15		10:15		10:15	10:15
	10:30		10:30		10:30		10:30	10:30
	10:45		10:45		10:45		10:45	10:45
11:00	11:00	11:00	11:00	11:00	11:00	11:00	11:00	11:00
	11:15		11:15		11:15		11:15	11:15
	11:30		11:30		11:30		11:30	11:30
	11:45		11:45		11:45		11:45	11:45
12:00	12:00	12:00	12:00	12:00	12:00	12:00	12:00	12:00

REFLECTIONS
on Priority Management

Setting priorities is a skill that you will need for the rest of your life. By learning to avoid procrastinating and taking the time to enhance the quality of your life, you are actually increasing your staying power as a college student. Further, as you enter the world of work, both of these skills will be necessary for your success. Technological advances, fewer people doing more work, and pressure to perform at unprecedented levels can put your life in a tailspin, but with the ability to plan your time, simplify your life, say "no," and find time for joy, you are making a contribution to your own success.

Knowledge in Bloom

MANAGING YOUR TIME

Each lesson-end assessment is based on Bloom's Taxonomy of Learning. See the first page of this lesson for a quick review.

This activity uses level 4 of the taxonomy

Think about the people at your school. With whom can you make a connection to learn more about priority management (for example, an instructor, counselor, advisor, retention specialist, etc.)? Why and how will this connection be important?

_____

_____

REFERENCES

Waitley, D. (1997). *Psychology of Success: Developing Your Self-Esteem*. Boston, MA: Irwin Career Education Division.

Babauta, L. (2012). Simple living manifesto: 72 ways to simplify your life. ZenHabits. Retrieved May 23, 2012, from http://zenhabits.net/simple-living-manifesto-72-ideas-to-simplify-your-life.

PROSPER

UNDERSTANDING AND USING FINANCIAL LITERACY

Rafael Ramirez Lee/iStockphoto

"It's good to have money and the things money can buy, but it's good, too, to check up once in a while and make sure you haven't lost the things that money can't buy."
—George Lorimer

Why read this lesson?

Because you'll learn how to:

- Create long- and short-term financial goals

Because you'll be able to:

- Define financial literacy
- Explain the advantages of setting financial goals
- Use strategies for managing your finances
- Recognize the advantages and disadvantages of using credit

Knowledge in Bloom

Bloom's Taxonomy of Learning is a simple way of explaining the levels at which we all learn material and acquire information. The learning levels progress from basic to more complex learning and thinking. Examples are detailed below. Throughout this lesson, you'll see colorful triangles to the side of some activities. They let you know on which level of Bloom's Taxonomy the questions are based.

- **LEVEL 1: Remember**
  Define financial literacy.
- **LEVEL 2: Understand**
  Summarize the steps in setting financial goals.
- **LEVEL 3: Apply**
  Apply strategies for managing your credit card debt.
- **LEVEL 4: Analyze**
  Analyze your daily expense log.
- **LEVEL 5: Evaluate**
  Validate your FICO score.
- **LEVEL 6: Create**
  Create a budget.

MyStudentSuccessLab

MyStudentSuccessLab is an online solution designed to help you acquire and develop (or hone) the skills you need to succeed. You will have access to peer-led video presentations and develop core skills through interactive exercises and projects.

TAKING CONTROL OF YOUR MONEY

Why Is It So Important to Understand Financial Literacy?

Exactly what is **financial literacy**? The President's Advisory Council on Financial Literacy (2008) defines personal financial literacy as "the ability to use knowledge and skills to manage financial resources effectively for a lifetime of financial well-being". Becoming financially literate, however, entails much more than just being able to balance your checkbook, plan a budget, or open a savings account. Financial literacy also encompasses the ability to plan for a successful future, to write long- and short-term financial goals, and to manage your finances in ways that allow you to take care of yourself and your family. Financial literacy includes making sound decisions relative to money management at every stage of your life, starting now. Some of the things you can do to become financially literate are: Read magazines like *Smart Money, Kiplinger's, and Money;* study books about investing; enroll in personal financial management courses; and ask questions of financially successful people. Arm yourself with knowledge and an understanding of financial terminology so you can take control of your own future.

> "To achieve the things you want, you need to understand your relationship with money, your belief system, and why you act the way you do."
> —Farnoosh Torabi

LEARNING TO SET FINANCIAL GOALS

Why Do People Fail to Plan Something So Important to Their Future?

Many, if not most, people spend more time deciding which television programs to watch every week than they do taking care of their financial future. Many people tend to drift from one day to the next, never stopping to look down the road or to think about what they would like to do and have. Your goals need to be measurable, realistic, and attainable, and they need to have deadlines. You may not always reach your goals, but you are much more likely to accomplish more with goals than without them. Study the important steps below to learn to set financial goals.

- **The first step** in setting financial goals is to get control of your daily spending! Delayed gratification is crucial to financial success. This means that you delay spending money on things that give you instant pleasure and wait until you can afford them. You will never be financially secure if you spend mindlessly on worthless things that you will soon forget or if you charge too much on credit cards with high interest rates that get out of control.

- **The second step** is to decide exactly what you want to accomplish financially. Do you want to pay off your credit card debt? Save for a house? Plan for a vacation? Open an account for your children's college funds? Save for retirement?

- **The third step** is to decide which goals are short-term goals (less than a year), mid-level goals (one to three years), and long-term goals (five years or more). As with any goal, you need to be specific and you must set deadlines. Long-term goals can be broken down into mid-level and short-term goals to make the end result less overwhelming. For example, your long-term goal may be: I will save two million dollars for my retirement in forty years. The sooner you start, the better. A mid-level goal might be: At the end of five years, I will have saved a minimum of $22,000, including my earnings, in my retirement account. You may have a short-term goal like this one: I will save $3000 toward my retirement fund this year by having funds deducted from my pay check monthly, and I will invest it in medium-aggressive stocks.

> *"Most people don't plan to fail; they just fail to plan."*
> —John L. Beckley

■ **The fourth step** is to evaluate your progress on a regular basis. Becoming financially secure is not something you can put on automatic pilot and forget about it. Like anything worth having, financial security requires hard work and, in the beginning, a certain amount of sacrifice. Goals should be monitored carefully and adjusted as needed.

Using the chart in Figure 3.1, create three short-term financial goals that you can reasonably attain within one year. Two examples are provided for you.

Level 6 Create

Figure 3.1 Creating Financial Goals

GOAL	TIME REQUIRED	AMOUNT	MONTHLY BUDGET	STRATEGY
Pay off my American Express credit card	12 months	$600	$60	Stop charging; put my card away and only use it for emergencies
Save $1000 for down payment on a car	6 months	$1000	$170	Get a part-time job; cut back on lattes; eat lunch at home

STRATEGIES FOR MANAGING YOUR FINANCES

What Does It Take to Become Financially Secure?

There are many smart people who make huge amounts of money and still end up with very little retirement savings. They spend and spend like there is no day of reckoning; trust your authors—a day of reckoning is coming. You can be financially secure and have enough money

Figure 3.2 Daily Expense Log

Use this log to keep track of every penny you spend.

DATE	EXPENSE	AMOUNT: CASH OR CHECK	AMOUNT: CREDIT	NECESSARY OR FRIVOLOUS?	COMMENTS:	WHAT I SHOULD HAVE DONE DIFFERENTLY?

to travel and enjoy life or you can end up scrimping and doing without and working at a part-time job when you are in your seventies when you could be playing golf or doing something else you would like to do. The answer is educating yourself about financial matters; making a strategically sound plan; and sticking to that plan. Study the following list for four of the most important strategies in financial management that can help you reach your goals:

CORNERSTONES OF FINANCIAL STRATEGIES

- Keep a **daily expense log** for a few weeks and determine exactly where your money is being spent. Analyze this log and determine how you can cut costs and save money. Copy and use the log in Figure 3.2 to track your expenses for at least two weeks.

- Construct a **budget** that includes all your income and fixed expenses (items that do not change from month to month, such as rent, car payment, etc.). A budget will show you where you have to spend money as well as how much you can spend on **discretionary spending** (the amount of money you have left over for saving, spending, and investing after you have paid all expenses). How you spend discretionary income is the difference in being financially secure and being broke. Complete a budget using the budget planner in Figure 3.3. Used properly, a budget planner can help you get control of your money.

- Manage your **credit card debt.** This is the worst kind of debt, and it is so easy to charge today and think you will be able to pay it off later. Imagine that you buy a $16 pizza on credit and are still paying for it twelve years later. This happens more than you can imagine. College students are credit card companies' dream customers. Take credit cards out of your wallet, and put them in a secure location. Use them only when you absolutely have to.

Can you imagine paying for a piece of pizza for 12 years?
Stacey Newman/iStockPhoto

Figure 3.3 Personal Budget Planner

CATEGORY	MONTHLY (DIVIDE BY 12)	COMMENTS
Savings		
Housing		
Food (includes groceries, lunches, snacks, eating out)		
Transportation (includes car payments, gas/oil)		
Automobile Insurance		
Automotive Maintenance Fees, Repairs, Tolls		
Public Transportation		
Telephone—Cell		
Telephone—Home		
Utilities (electricity, gas, water, sewer)		
Internet/Cable		
Loans		
Credit Cards		
Medical Expenses		
Dental Expenses		
Fitness (gym, yoga, massage)		
Entertainment		
Vacations		
Pets (food, veterinarian, grooming)		
Daycare (if you have children)		
Education		
Clothing		
Insurance		
Miscellaneous (toiletries, household products, grooming, hair, makeup)		

- **Control student loan debt.** Many students leave college with huge student loan debts. Although you may have to borrow money to attend college, you can still minimize what you owe by making smart decisions. Don't take money you don't need, and graduate as quickly as you can to reduce your debt.
- **Save for emergencies.** Employed people are advised to save at least six months' salary in case they have emergencies or lose their jobs. Open a savings account and put a set amount in this account every month until you have enough saved that you feel secure. This is an excellent financial habit to establish now that will serve you well later.

DAILY EXPENSE LOG

Where Does the Money Go?

One of the best ways to get a handle on how you are spending your money is to keep a **Daily Expense Log.** This means writing down every penny you spend, so it takes discipline! After you have done this for at least two weeks, you will be able to pinpoint exactly where your money is going and how you are wasting your funds. Use the Daily Expense Log in Figure 3.2 to track your expenses.

YOUR PERSONAL BUDGET PLANNER

Are Budgets Really Important?

Now that you understand how important planning, analyzing, managing, and saving are to your financial success and to your long-term future, construct a budget using the form in Figure 3.3. You will most likely need to adjust this budget as you become more in touch with how you are spending your money.

ADVANTAGES AND DISADVANTAGES OF CREDIT

What's the Score?

Credit, in and of itself, is not necessarily a bad thing. You actually need to establish a credit rating that you can use when you want to purchase a car or buy a house or any number of other important items. What you don't want to do is get deep in debt, default on your debt, and end up with a very bad credit score. You need to know the score—the FICO score! FICO stands for Fair Isaac Corporation. Financial guru Suze Orman (2007) says, "Just about every financial move you will make for the rest of your life will be somehow linked to your FICO score. Not knowing how your score is calculated, how it is used, and how you can improve it will keep you broke long past your young-and-fabulous days. The way the business world sees it, your FICO score is a great tool to size up how good you will be at handling a new loan or a credit card, or whether you're a solid citizen to rent an apartment to." If you have a high FICO score, you will get better interest rates. Your FICO score can impact everything from your ability to finance a house to being able to get reasonable automobile insurance premiums.

Know Your FICO!

So, what is this thing called a **FICO score**? This carefully researched information based on your credit history, income, and ability to repay your debts is a score that determines your level of future credit risk. Your FICO score is a three-digit number based on your bill-paying history and is an important component of your overall financial profile. In general, a credit score can range from a low of 300 to a high of 850. Most scores fall in the 600 or 700 range (Consumers Union Organization, 2007). "Generally speaking, a score of 750 or higher is considered in the top tier. Anything below 650 is at the other end of the spectrum" (Slade, 2011). How important is all of this? The Consumer Federation of America estimates that someone with a bad credit score would be charged $5000 more than someone with a good score on a five-year $20,000 car loan (Slade, 2011). Study the suggestions listed in Figure 3.4 for assistance in managing your credit.

Figure 3.4 **Cornerstones for Managing Your Credit**

- **Only borrow and spend what you can afford.** Never live beyond your means because this takes away your freedom.
- **Try to pay bills as soon as they arrive.** A late payment on one account can cost you higher rates and fees on all your other unrelated accounts!
- **Pay credit card bills in full each month,** or at least pay more than the minimum amount due.
- **Call and have the due date changed** if a payment falls at a time of the month when you may be short on cash.
- **Avoid special services that credit card lenders may offer** like fraud protection, insurance, travel club, etc. Avoid free trial offers that are billed automatically to your credit card if you forget to cancel.
- **Use the services of PRBC (Pay Rent, Build Credit) to build a payment history.** Once you enroll, PRBC will keep a payment history of your rental, utility, and other recurring bill payments and provide that information to the three credit reporting bureaus.
- **Check your credit report every year** for accuracy and dispute inaccurate information immediately.

Source: Adapted from State of New York Banking Department (2011).

CREDIT CARD DEBT

What Is the "Fox in the Hen House"?

Credit card companies' dream customers are college students. In many cases, students know very little about credit; they don't have a lot of cash so they frequently get themselves deep in debt. So beware of strangers bearing gifts in the form of credit card applications—they are the "fox in the hen house."

While credit card debt can still wreak havoc on your financial position, some of the new legal changes are a great improvement. The new laws include the following:

- Credit card companies cannot change fees, terms, or interest rates without a 45-day notice.

- Payments must come due on the same day every month.

- Credit card companies must provide information that details how long it will take you to pay a debt if you pay only the minimum. (Pay attention to this one!)

- The credit card company cannot change your interest rate during the first year you have the card. If the rate is 13 percent, for example, when you open the account, it cannot change for a year unless it is an introductory rate (beware of these) or if you are more than 60 days late in paying your bill.

- Interest rate increases can only be applied to new charges; your old charges will still carry the same rate as before. (Adapted from Torabi, Farnoosh. (n.d.). "New Credit Card Laws Take Effect." Retrieved from www.farnoosh.tv/financial-basics/debt-management/new-credit-card-laws-take-effect.)

How many credit cards do you currently have? Do you use them wisely?
Nick M. Do/iStockPhoto

If you fall into the credit card trap of making only the minimum payment and you continue to rack up large bills, you will soon find yourself in a deep hole, and it is very hard to dig out. If you make a late payment, you have really compounded the problem because your credit card company will immediately raise your interest rate. Not only will that specific credit card company raise your interest rate, all the other companies with which you have credit cards might also raise your rates.

An even worse scenario is to charge the maximum on several credit cards and to begin making only the minimum payment. Consider the following scenario.

> If you continue making partial payments, the interest charges are calculated on the new credit card debt. So you end up paying interest on the last month's interest, too. Thus your credit card debt accumulates rapidly and soon you find that what was once a relatively small amount of credit card debt has ballooned into a big amount, which you find almost impossible to pay. Moreover, if you don't control your spending habits, your credit card debt rises even faster. This is how the vicious circle of credit card debt works. (Geyer, 2011)

The only way to get off the credit card merry-go-round is to stop charging, pay more than the minimum, and try to get the credit card company to lower your interest rate. Call the credit card company and ask to speak to a supervisor and insist on a lower rate.

Be wary of **credit counseling services**. These companies offer to help you get out of credit card debt by negotiating on your behalf with your creditors. "It is wise to seek credit counseling through a service accredited by the Association of Independent Consumer Credit Counseling Agencies or the National Foundation for Credit Counseling. It is far less likely that an accredited organization will charge excessive fees or try to take advantage of you, than it is for an organization which is not accredited" (Larson, 2011).

Study the list of suggestions in Figure 3.5 for checking out credit card companies before you sign up.

> "If you are making the minimum payments on $20,000 in credit card debt at 8%, it will take you 23.5 years to pay it off. At 19% (US average), it would take you 46 years."
> —Opportunity Debt Management

Figure 3.5 Check It Out!

Before accepting a credit card, check the following items carefully:

- Look for the lowest permanent interest rate.
- Look for credit cards with low or no annual fees. If you will pay your credit card bill off every month, no annual fee is important.
- Don't accept a credit card simply because you can get it or if you are offered a high credit limit. Avoid having too many cards.
- Read the terms of the credit card offer as well as the disclosure statement that comes with a card. Check for annual fees, late payment fees, over-the-limit fees, account setup fees, cash advance fees, and the method they use to calculate balances.
- Be careful of low introductory rates. These special rates can last for short periods of times, and then skyrocket once the introductory period is over if you are late with a payment.
- Call the issuer and make sure they report to a credit agency—you want any positive payment history that you build to be reflected in your credit report.

Comparative credit card rates can be found on the New York State Banking Department's Website and are available to consumers for free.

Source: Adapted from State of New York Banking Department (2011).

WHAT YOU NEED TO KNOW ABOUT STUDENT LOANS

Why Do So Many Students Feel That They Are Majoring in Debt?

The high cost of college makes tuition out of reach for many, if not most, families. For many students, the only way they can attend college is by using student loans. If this is the only way you can go to college, borrow the money—but **borrow no more than you absolutely must.** Unlike other forms of financial aid, education loans must be repaid with interest. Still, most students use loans to help pay for college. If you're unable to meet all your college costs through other means like scholarships, current family income, and savings, then saying yes to a college loan is a smart move.

Student Loan Borrowing Tips

Wise borrowers keep these tips about student loans in mind so that they graduate with as little debt as possible:

- Borrow only what you need to cover education expenses. You don't have to borrow the full amount offered in the financial aid award letter.
- Consider working while in school.
- Look for ways to keep living costs down, such as having a roommate, using a budget, and packing your lunch.
- Try to finish your college education in the fastest time possible. Every term means another student loan.

Have you allotted enough time in your schedule to fill out your financial aid application completely and accurately?
Bob Daemmrich/PhotoEdit

from ordinary to

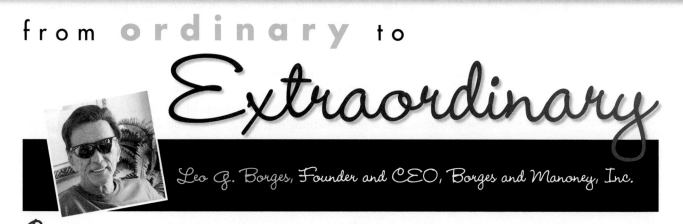

Extraordinary

Leo G. Borges, Founder and CEO, Borges and Manoney, Inc.

Can the son of an immigrant, born in a rural area detached from the rest of the world, become financially successful? Absolutely yes! And Leo Borges proved it. When Leo was only three years old, his father passed away, and when he was eleven, his mother died. He lived with and was raised by his sisters, but he was not able to shed the feelings of insecurity. Leo's primary feelings when he was growing up were aloneness and isolation. He and his siblings were orphans; they were poor; they were farm kids; and they were Portuguese—not Americans. There was never a day in his life that someone did not remind him of these realities. Leo clung to the fact that his mother had always told him and his siblings that they could be anything or have anything if they believed in it and worked hard for it.

> *He and his siblings were orphans; they were poor; they were farm kids; and they were Portuguese—not Americans.*

Leo moved to San Francisco to attend a program in advertising when he was 17. Later that year he moved to Los Angeles and began working for a major advertising company. He enlisted in the Coast Guard and later worked for an oil company and then a major leasing firm. When he was in his early forties, he and his best friend started their own business in the water treatment industry. Leo was an excellent salesman and Cliff was an excellent accountant so by using their talents, conducting careful research, and working hard, they started a small store-front in San Francisco, but they grew and grew. Before they sold their very successful business twenty years later, they had 15 full-time employees and annual revenues in the millions of dollars. He moved from ordinary to extraordinary!

EXTRAORDINARY REFLECTION

Leo Borges could have allowed difficult times and deprivation to destroy his chances of being successful and happy. Instead he used his trials and tribulations to make him stronger and more determined to succeed. What difficulties do you need to overcome in order to be the successful person you were meant to be?

It's also a good idea to keep close track of your loan debt and, when possible, avoid borrowing from multiple programs and lenders (College Board, 2011).

More Things You Need to Know about Student Loans

According to Torabi (2011), the median student loan debt is at record levels due to rising tuition costs, and has now reached an average of $34,000; many students owe much more than this. If you are one of the many students who borrowed money to go to college, you are probably concerned about your ability to repay the loans while maintaining a good quality of life after you graduate. Before you graduate or transfer, find out everything you need to know about your loan, and determine your options. Some of the most pertinent points about student loans are as follows.

- You have a legal obligation to repay your student loans with interest.
- Bankruptcy will not eliminate your obligation to repay any student loans.

- You should get the addresses and phone numbers of lenders before you leave college. Certain circumstances, such as graduate school, allow you to defer your payments. A **deferment** allows you to postpone your payments, but you will still have to pay these loans with interest.

- Learn all the options you have for repaying your loans. Based on your salary, expenses, and budget, decide which one is best for you. Do this **before** you leave school!

- If for some reason you cannot make your payment, let the lender know immediately. This is not something that will go away. You do not want to default on your loan, as this will cause you to have a bad credit rating, prohibit you from holding a government job, and prohibit you from getting a tax refund until the loan is repaid.

- If possible, consolidate your loans while you are in your grace period (six months after you graduate) because the interest rate will be lower.

- Complete your consolidation application and send it in before June 30 if possible because interest rates are most likely to increase on July 1.

REFLECTIONS on Financial Literacy

Some of the points mentioned throughout this book will have a major impact on your life and your lifestyle, but none will be more important than making wise financial management decisions. These decisions include daily budgeting, using an expense log, and making smart credit card choices. Making the right financial decisions requires taking time to educate yourself about the options. Prepare yourself to make wise financial decisions!

Knowledge in Bloom

PROTECT YOURSELF FROM IDENTITY THEFT

Each lesson-end assessment is based on Bloom's Taxonomy of Learning. See the first page of this lesson for a quick review.

This activity uses levels 2–6 of the taxonomy

The FBI calls identity theft one of the fastest-growing crimes in the United States and reports that 500,000 to 700,000 Americans are victims each year. Identity theft is a federal crime that happens when someone assumes another person's identity. This occurs when someone's name, social security number, or any account number is used for unlawful activities (Federal Reserve Bank of Boston, 2011). Identity thieves frequently open new accounts in someone else's name. They often apply for new credit cards using another person's information, make charges, and leave the bills unpaid. **Identify theft is a serious problem for victims!** Complete the exercise that follows to learn more about protecting yourself from identity theft.

First, access a website about protecting oneself from identity theft. Summarize the main points in the space below.

_____

_____

_____

_____

_____

_____

_____

_____

_____

_____

_____

_____

_____

Now, design a strategy for protecting yourself from identity theft.

_____

_____

_____

_____

_____

_____

_____

_____

_____

_____

_____

_____

_____

_____

REFERENCES

College Board. (2011). Student loan comparison calculator: Private/alternative loans. Retrieved March 15, 2011, from http://apps.collegeboard.com/loancompare/loancomparisonintro.jsp.

Consumers Union Organization. (2007). What is a credit score? Retrieved April 17, 2007, from www.consumersunion.org/creditmatters/creditmattersfactsheet/001633.html.

Federal Reserve Bank of Boston. (2011). Identity theft. Retrieved from www.bostonfed.org.

Geyer, Joseph. (2011). "What Is Credit Card Debt?" Retrieved March 15, 2011, from http://hubpages.com/hub/What-is-Credt-Card-Debt.

Larson, Aaron. (2011). Expert law website. Finding a good credit counseling service. Retrieved April 10, 2011, from www.expertlaw.com/library/finance/good_credit_counselor.html.

Orman, Suze. (2007). *The Money Book for the Young, Fabulous, and Broke.* New York, NY: Riverhead Books.

President's Advisory Council on Financial Literacy. (2008). Annual Report to the President.

Slade, David. (2011, March). Don't gamble with your credit score. *The State*, p. B-4.

State of New York Banking Department. (2011). Using credit wisely: What you need to know. Retrieved March 16, 2011, from www.banking.state.ny.us/brcw.htm.

Torabi, Farnoosh. (2011). Presentation at Pearson's Conference. Savannah, Georgia.

Torabi, Farnoosh. (n.d.). New credit card laws take effect. Retrieved from www.farnoosh.tv/financial-basics/debt-management/new-credit-card-laws-take-effect

THINK

DEVELOPING YOUR CRITICAL AND CREATIVE THINKING SKILLS

"Many people think they are thinking when they are merely rearranging their prejudices." —William James

THINK

Why read this lesson?

Because you'll learn how to:

- Solve a problem using critical and creative thinking

Because you'll be able to:

- Analyze steps in the critical thinking process
- Explain the value of using critical and creative thinking skills to solve problems
- Learn the process of making a logical, rational decision
- Use creative thinking techniques

Knowledge in Bloom

Bloom's Taxonomy of Learning is a simple way of explaining the levels at which we all learn material and acquire information. The learning levels progress from basic to more complex learning and thinking. Examples are detailed below. Throughout this lesson, you'll see colorful triangles to the side of some activities. They let you know on which level of Bloom's Taxonomy the questions are based.

- **LEVEL 1: Remember**
  Define critical thinking.
- **LEVEL 2: Understand**
  Discuss how critical thinking can be used.
- **LEVEL 3: Apply**
  Solve a school-related problem.
- **LEVEL 4: Analyze**
  Test your knowledge of the problem-solving process.
- **LEVEL 5: Evaluate**
  Evaluate potential solutions to one of your biggest challenges.
- **LEVEL 6: Create**
  Create a plan for managing your emotions using emotional intelligence (EI) skills.

MyStudentSuccessLab

MyStudentSuccessLab is an online solution designed to help you acquire and develop (or hone) the skills you need to succeed. You will have access to peer-led video presentations and develop core skills through interactive exercises and projects.

THE IMPORTANCE
OF CRITICAL THINKING

Is It Ever Used? Really?

Have you ever made a decision that turned out to be a mistake? Have you ever said to yourself, *"If only I could go back and ..."* Have you ever regretted actions you took toward a person or situation? Have you ever planned a paper or speech that was flawless? Have you ever had to make a hard, painful decision that turned out to be "the best decision of your life"? If the answer to any of these questions is yes, you might be able to trace the consequences back to your ***thought process*** at the time of the decision. Let's face it, sometimes good and bad things just happen out of luck or circumstance. More often than not, however, many events in our lives are driven by the thought processes involved when we made the initial decision and chose to act on those decisions.

Critical thinking can serve us in many areas as students and citizens in a free society. ***Critical thinking can help you:***

- Focus on relevant issues/problems and avoid wasting time on the trivial
- Gather relevant, accurate information regarding finances, goals, decision making, relationships, civic responsibility, and environmental issues, to name a few
- Understand and remember facts and organize thoughts logically
- Look more deeply at problems, analyze their causes, and solve them more accurately
- Develop appropriate and meaningful study plans and manage your priorities
- Assist in your problem-solving skills
- Help you control your emotions so that you can make rational judgments and become more open-minded
- Produce new knowledge through research and analysis
- Help you determine the accuracy of printed and spoken words
- Assist you in detecting bias and determining the relevance of arguments and persuasion

THE FOUR STEPS
TO CRITICAL THINKING

Can Critical Thinking Work in Everyday Life?

Does critical thinking really matter? Seriously? Can it do anything to improve the quality of your life? The answer is yes. Critical thinking has daily, practical uses, from making sound financial decisions to improving personal relationships to helping you become a better student to helping you make a good deal on purchasing a car. You can improve your critical thinking skills by watching your emotional reactions, using solid research and facts to build your thoughts, and practicing open-mindedness.

As you begin to build and expand your critical-thinking skills, consider the following steps, also shown in Figure 4.1.

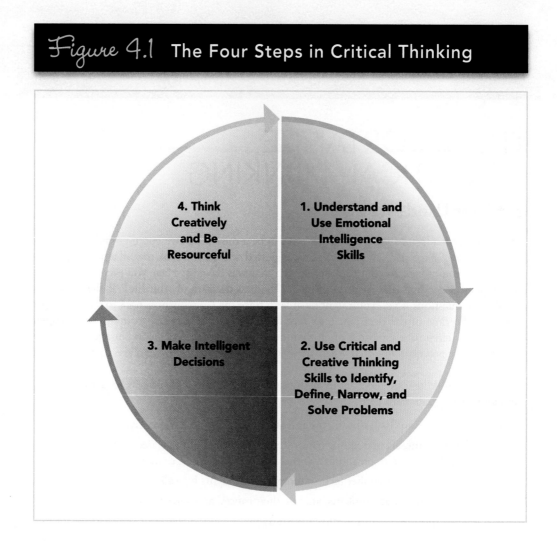

Figure 4.1 The Four Steps in Critical Thinking

4. Think Creatively and Be Resourceful

1. Understand and Use Emotional Intelligence Skills

3. Make Intelligent Decisions

2. Use Critical and Creative Thinking Skills to Identify, Define, Narrow, and Solve Problems

STEP ONE: UNDERSTAND AND USE EMOTIONAL INTELLIGENCE SKILLS

Emotions play a vital role in our lives. They help us feel compassion, help us help others, help us reach out in times of need, and help us relate to others. Emotions can, on the other hand, cause some problems in your critical-thinking process. You do not and should not have to eliminate emotions from your thoughts, but it is crucial that you know when your emotions are clouding an issue and causing you to act and speak before thinking.

Consider the following topics:

- Should drugs and prostitution be completely legalized in the United States?
- Can the theories of evolution and creationism coexist?
- Should illegal aliens be given amnesty and made U.S. citizens?
- Should the legal drinking age be lowered to 18?
- Should terminally ill patients have the right to assisted suicide?

As you read these topics, did you immediately form an opinion? Did old arguments surface? Did you feel your emotions coming into play as you thought about the questions? If you had an immediate answer, it is likely that you allowed some past judgments, opinions, and emotions to enter the decision-making process unless you have just completed a comprehensive, unbiased study of one of these issues. If you had to discuss these issues in class or with your friends and had to defend your position, how would you react? Do you think you would get angry? Would you find yourself groping for words? Would you find it hard to explain why you held the opinion that you voiced? If so, these are warning signs that you are allowing your emotions to drive your decisions. If you allow your emotions to run rampant (not using restraint) and fail to use research, logic, and evidence, you may not be able to examine the issues critically or have a logical discussion regarding the statements.

SHARPENING YOUR EMOTIONAL INTELLIGENCE (EI) SKILLS

How Does EI Affect Critical Thinking and Problem Solving?

If you have ever heard the old saying, "THINK before you act," you were actually being told to use *emotional intelligence.* Everyone knows that **IQ** (Intelligence Quotient) is important to success in college, work, and life, but many experts also believe that **EI** (emotional intelligence) is just as important to being successful. Emotional intelligence helps people cope with the social and emotional demands in daily life. "Emotional intelligence is the single most influencing variable in personal achievement, career success, leadership, and life satisfaction" (Nelson and Low, 2003). "The data that exist suggest it can be *as powerful*, and at times *more powerful*, than IQ" (Goleman, 2006).

"Simply stated, people who are emotionally intelligent harness emotions and work with them to improve problem solving and boost creativity."
—Snyder and Lopez (2007)

Exactly what is EI? EI includes all the skills and knowledge necessary for building strong, effective relationships through managing and understanding emotions. *It is knowing how **you** and **others** understand and manage feelings and emotions in a rational manner that is good for both parties.* Consider Figure 4.2 (adapted from Snyder and Lopez, 2007).

Our emotions originate in the brain. If you have emotional intelligence skills, your ***thinking mind*** and ***emotional mind*** should function together, making it more likely that you will craft sound, rational decisions. In other words, you will **think** before you **act**. When these two minds do not operate in harmony, you might say things, do things, and make highly emotional decisions that can be viewed as irrational.

STEP TWO: USE CRITICAL AND CREATIVE THINKING SKILLS TO IDENTIFY, DEFINE, NARROW, AND SOLVE PROBLEMS

What would your life be like if you had no problems? Most people do not like to face or deal with problems, but the critical thinker knows that problems exist every day and that they must be faced and solved. Some of our problems are larger and more difficult than others, but we all face problems from time-to-time. You may have transportation problems. You may have financial problems. You may have childcare problems. You may have academic problems or interpersonal problems. There are many ways to address and solve problems. In this section, we will discuss how to *identify and narrow* the problem, *research and develop* alternatives, *evaluate* the alternatives, and **solve** the problem.

Figure 4.2   Emotional Intelligence Chart

Perceiving Emotions

- Identify emotions in other people, such as facial expressions and vocal tones
- Express your emotions clearly and accurately
- Detect authentic and inauthentic emotions in yourself and others

Using Emotions Wisely to Clarify Your Thoughts

- Use your emotions and feelings wisely and appropriately
- Generate appropriate emotions to facilitate responses
- Use emotions to critically and creatively solve problems

Understanding Emotions

- Understand relationships among various emotions
- Perceive and interpret the causes and consequences of emotions over time
- Understand complex feelings and contradictory emotions in yourself and others

Managing Emotions

- Be open to feelings, both pleasant and unpleasant
- Monitor and reflect on your emotions and others' emotions
- Manage and regulate emotions (even negative emotions) in oneself and others

Source: Adapted from Snyder and Lopez (2007).

By using your critical and creative thinking skills, you will be able to solve many problems through research, logic, reason, and, sometimes, through developing ideas that have not been used before. By taking the time to critically and creatively think about the root of a problem, possible solutions, and new, imaginative endings, the time spent thinking before acting will serve you well in your studies and in the world of work.

Consider the problem-solving model in Figure 4.3.

Identify the *Symptoms*

Symptoms and *problems* are not the same thing. Symptoms are *part* of the problem, but may not be the problem itself. Think of a problem like you think of your health. For example, you may have aches in your joints, experience cold chills, and have a severe headache. These seem like problems, but in actuality, they are really symptoms of something larger— perhaps the flu or an infection. You can treat the headache with medicine, and soothe your joint pain with ointment, but until you get at the *root* of the problem, these symptoms will come back.

Narrow the Symptoms to Find the *Root Problem*

Often, problems keep coming up because we did not deal with the *real problem*—the root problem—but, rather, we dealt with a symptom. Getting to the heart of a problem is hard work and requires a great deal of thought, research, and patience. Begin by putting

Figure 4.3   Steps in the Problem-Solving Process

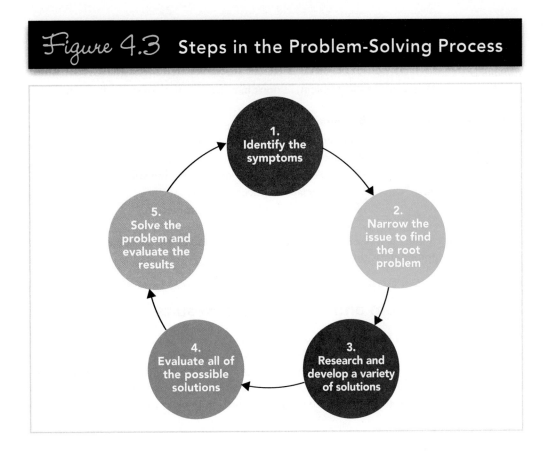

your symptoms in writing, perhaps on notecards so that you can lay them out and see them all at once. When doing this, be sure to jot down all of the major and minor symptoms, such as:

- What are the daily challenges that keep coming up?
- Who is involved?
- How are the symptoms hindering your overall goals?
- Who or what is responsible for creating these symptoms?

Research and Develop a Variety of *Solutions*

It is a mistake to try to solve a problem when you don't have enough information to do so. It may be that you need to conduct interviews, research what others who face similar issues have done, read current data and reports, or even explore historical documents. Paul and Elder (2006) suggest that the type of information you need is determined by the type of problem you have and the question(s) you are trying to answer. "If you have a historical question, you need *historical information*. If you have a biological question, you need *biological information*. If you have an ethical question, you must identify at least one relevant *ethical principle*." Therefore, part of the problem-solving process is to gather your facts—the correct facts—before you try to reach a resolution.

Evaluate and Analyze All of the *Possible* Solutions

After you have gathered your research (through formal methods and/or brainstorming) you must now evaluate your solutions to determine which would work best and why.

After careful study and deliberation, without emotional interference, analyze the solutions you came up with and determine if they are appropriate or inappropriate. To analyze, create Columns A and B. Write the *possible solutions in Column A* and an evaluative *comment in Column B.*

An example follows using the problem, "I don't have enough time to study due to my job":

A (Possible Solutions)	B (Comments)
Quit the job.	Very hard to do. I need the money for tuition and car.
Cut my hours at work.	Will ask my boss.
Find a new job.	Hard to do because of the job market—but will look into it.
Get a student loan.	Visit financial aid office tomorrow.
Quit school.	No—it is my only chance for a promotion.

With your comments in Column B, you can now begin to eliminate some of the alternatives that are inappropriate at this time.

Solve the Problem and *Evaluate* the *Results*

Now that you have a few strong possible solutions, you have some work to do. You will need to talk to your boss, go to the financial aid office, and possibly begin to search for a new job with flexible hours. Basically, you are creating a *plan* to bring this solution to life. After you have researched each possible solution further, you will be able to make a decision based on solid information and facts. You will be able to figure out which solution is the best option for you.

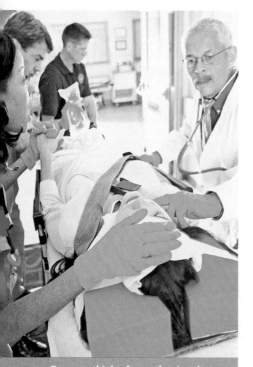

STEP THREE: MAKE INTELLIGENT DECISIONS

You make decisions every day. These decisions may be small, such as, "What am I going to have for lunch?" or large decisions, like, "Should I change jobs in this economy?" There are many factors that influence our decisions, such as our past experiences, our tolerance for risk, our comfort level, our desire to change, and our relationships with others. To further complicate the issue of decision making, we are faced with immediacy. In today's information-centered world, we seldom have time to sit back and digest all of the facts and angles before we're required to make life-altering decisions. Because of the pace at which decision making is required in today's world, we sometimes add two and two together and get five (MindTools, 2011).

One of the most effective ways to make a decision is to use a numerical scale to actually assign a "grade" to each choice before you. Consider the following example and Figure 4.4 of having to make a decision between two jobs.

- **Create an Element column.** This column lists the aspects of the job that are important to you, such as pay, potential for growth, benefits, joy of work, etc. You should make up this list based on what you need and value.

- **Create a Rating of Importance column.** This column gives each element a rating that you assign. Using a scale of 1 to 10, you will decide if pay or benefits are very important in your new job (an 8, 9, or 10) or not very important (a 1, 2, or 3).

- **Create a Choice #1 column**. This column will list the numerical calculations for your first job choice. You will decide how important each item in column one is, and then you will give it a rating based on your research about both jobs. Then multiply that number by your importance rating.

- **Create a Choice #2 column**. This column will list the numerical calculations for your second job choice. You will decide how important each item in column one is, and then you will give it a rating based on your research about both jobs. Then multiply that number by your importance rating.

Once you have created your columns (see Figure 4.4), you will work through your decisions using your head and your heart.

As you can see, Mercy Hospital is the best choice based on Samantha's list of things she values in a job. A numerical score may not be the ultimate in decision making, but at least you have taken the time to think about what is important to you, what is offered within the choices, and how it ranks in importance to you. By using this system, you are calling on your head and your heart to make decisions that could impact your life for a very long time.

Figure 4.4   Decision-Making Chart

The following example shows a decision-making chart between two job offers for Samantha. The Element column lists the items that are most important to Samantha in selecting a new job. The second column assigns a number to the element based on Samantha's values and that element's importance to her. The third and fourth columns rate the actual job's ranking based on Samantha's column two. For example, Samantha rated "distance to work from home" as an eight (very important). However, for the job at Mercy, she gives this element a five (only moderate), and at Grace, she rates it at a two (poor).

ELEMENT I VALUE IN MY JOB	MY RATING OF IMPORTANCE 1–10	CHOICE 1 JOB AT MERCY HOSPITAL	CHOICE 2 JOB AT GRACE HOSPITAL
Distance to work from home	8	My Rating = 5 8 x 5 = 40	My Rating = 2 2 x 8 = 16
Pay	10	My Rating = 9 10 x 9 = 90	My Rating = 7 10 x 7 = 70
Benefits	9	My Rating = 2 9 x 2 = 18	My Rating = 7 9 x 7 = 63
Potential for growth	5	My Rating = 5 5 x 5 = 25	My Rating = 5 5 x 5 = 25
Upgraded facility	7	My Rating = 6 7 x 6 = 42	My Rating = 4 7 x 4 = 28
		TOTAL SCORE = 215	TOTAL SCORE = 202

from ordinary to

Extraordinary

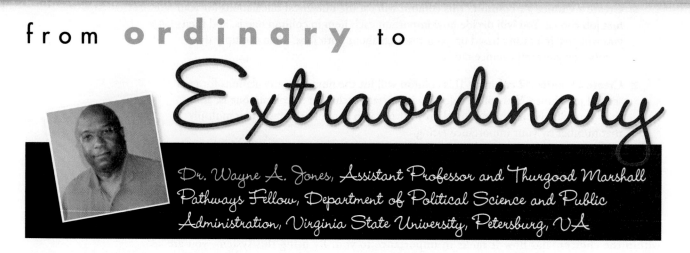

Dr. Wayne A. Jones, Assistant Professor and Thurgood Marshall Pathways Fellow, Department of Political Science and Public Administration, Virginia State University, Petersburg, VA

Dr. Jones comes from a fine family. His mother is a retired social worker, college professor, and community activist, and his father is a retired Presbyterian minister and college professor. They provided a safe, structured environment and always encouraged him to do well. Clearly he had the foundation to do well in school. However, he did not always follow his parent's advice. This was especially true for his senior year in high school. The outcome of his bad decisions was that he did not graduate. So at 18, he started working, got his own apartment and things were OK for a while. At least, so he thought.

Dr. Jones had always been interested in anything that had wheels on it. If it had wheels, he wanted to drive it! He drove a school bus for a few years and then he drove an ambulance. Additionally, he had a part-time job driving a taxi. One day, however, he saw the local bookmobile and wanted to drive it as it was different from anything that he

had previously operated. He applied to do so, but found out that he had to have a high school diploma to be able to drive the bookmobile. At 19, this became his reason for going back to get a GED.

With his GED in hand, his parents encouraged him to begin his college studies. Subsequently, he enrolled at Virginia Commonwealth University. After only one year, he decided that college was not for him. He did not return for a third semester. In 1975, he began working for the Police Department in Chesterfield, VA. He was only the second African American police officer on the force. He held this position for four years.

His desire for wheels was still with him. He left the police department and began working for The Virginia Overland Transportation Company as a safety supervisor/bus driver. A short time later, he was promoted to Operations Manager. With this experience under his belt, he went

STEP FOUR: THINK CREATIVELY AND BE RESOURCEFUL

Creative thinking is a major, important aspect of critical thinking in that you are producing something that is uniquely yours—introducing something to the world that is new, innovative, and useful. Creative thinking does not mean that you have to be an artist, a musician, or a writer. Creative thinking means that you have examined a situation and developed a new way of explaining information, delivering a product, or using an item. It can be as simple as discovering that you can use a small rolling suitcase to carry your books around instead of a traditional backpack. Creative thinking means that you have opened your mind to possibilities! Creative thinking gives you the tools to find internal resourcefulness.

Your inner resourcefulness and creativity also make you more secure and offer more protection from outside forces. When you know how to make ends meet, you can always do it. When you know how to pay the rent on limited income, you can always do it. When you know how to cut firewood to heat your home, you can always do it. When you know how

to work for a larger bus company in Richmond, VA, driving a city transit bus. He left the second bus company after a year to begin driving for a local construction company. This work, however, turned out to be very "seasonal" and he found himself frequently without income. This company also operated trash trucks, so he asked to be allowed to drive one of their trash trucks so that he could have a steady income, and overtime, too. So, there he was, in his early 30s, without a college degree, driving either a dump truck or a trash truck. At his grandmother's urging, he decided to return to college.

In just a few short years, he went from driving a trash truck to being a university professor.

There he was, working full time, going to college full time and attending classes several nights a week, and studying on the nights that he did not have classes. One night, he received a phone call that changed his life. His parents called him and told him that they wanted to talk with him about his education. To his surprise, they asked him to quit work and concentrate on his studies. They told him that if he quit, they would help with the bills until he finished college. Dr. Jones agreed to take their help.

He transferred from John Tyler Community College and enrolled again at Virginia Commonwealth University and completed his bachelor's degree. Later, he went on to complete his Masters of Public Administration. He then applied to the doctoral program in higher education administration at George Washington University. They accepted him provisionally. However, he again rose to the occasion. His dissertation won the *Outstanding Dissertation of the Year Award* in 2000 from the George Washington University chapter of Phi Delta Kappa.

Upon completion of his doctorate, he saw an ad in the local newspaper for an adjunct teaching position. It was through this part-time position that he found the love of his life—teaching. He later applied to become a full-time faculty member at Virginia State University, and today he teaches Freshman Studies and Public Administration. He changed his life from ordinary to extraordinary.

EXTRAORDINARY REFLECTION

Dr. Jones was brave enough to take an enormous risk, quit his full-time job, accept help, and reach his goals. Who do you have in your life that you can depend upon for support (maybe not monetary support, but crucial support of your goals, dreams, and educational plans)? Why?

to navigate the public transportation system in your town, you can always do it—even when the time comes when you don't have to "do it" anymore, you could if you had to. The more you know and the more inner strength and resourcefulness you have, the safer you are against the unknown. The more confidence you possess, the greater the likelihood that you can survive any thing at any time. The more creativity and resourcefulness you have, the more you understand that these qualities will help you rebuild all that may have been lost. When the world **has** been handed to you on a silver platter, you cannot be ready for what the world **can** hand you.

To begin the creative process, consider the characteristics creative thinkers have in common shown in Figure 4.5.

Using your imaginative and innovative juices, think about how you would *creatively* solve the following problem. Write down at least five possibilities. Come on, make it count!

Figure 4.5   Characteristics of Creative Thinking

COMPASSION	Creative thinkers have a zest for life and genuinely care for the spirit of others.	*Example*: More than 40 years ago, community members who wanted to feed the elderly created Meals on Wheels, now a national organization feeding the elderly.
COURAGE	Creative thinkers are unafraid to try new things, to implement new thoughts and actions.	*Example*: An NBC executive moved the Today Show out of a closed studio onto the streets of New York, creating the number-one morning news show in America.
TRUTH	Creative thinkers search for the true meanings of things.	*Example*: The astronomer and scientist Copernicus sought to prove that Earth was not the center of the universe—an unpopular view at the time. He was correct.
DREAMS	Creative thinkers allow themselves time to dream and ponder the unknown. They can see what is possible, not just what is real.	*Example*: John F. Kennedy dreamed that space exploration was possible. His dream became reality.
RISK TAKING	Creative thinkers take positive risks every day. They are not afraid to go against popular opinion.	*Example*: Barack Obama took a risk and ran for President of the United States. He became one of only a few African Americans to ever run for the office and the only African American to be nominated by his party. In November of 2008, he became the first African American President of the United States.
INNOVATION	Creative thinkers find new ways to do old things.	*Example*: Instead of continuing to fill the earth with waste such as aluminum, plastic, metal, and old cars, means were developed to recycle these materials for future productive use.
COMPETITION	Creative thinkers strive to be better, to think bolder thoughts, to do what is good, and to be the best at any task.	*Example*: A textbook writer updates the publication every three years to include new and revised information so the product remains competitive.
INDIVIDUALITY	Creative thinkers are not carbon copies of other people. They strive to be true to themselves.	*Example*: A young man decides to take tap dancing instead of playing baseball. He excels and wins a fine arts dancing scholarship to college.
CURIOSITY	Creative thinkers are interested in all things; they want to know much about many things.	*Example*: A 65-year-old retired college professor goes back to college to learn more about music appreciation and computer programming to expand her possibilities.
PERSEVERANCE	Creative thinkers do not give up. They stick to a project to its logical and reasonable end.	*Example*: Dr. Martin Luther King Jr. did not give up on his dream in the face of adversity, danger, and death threats.

The Problem

Jennifer is a first-year student who does not have enough money to pay her tuition, buy her books, and purchase a few new outfits and shoes to wear to class and her work-study job.

What should she do? Should she pay her tuition and purchase her books, or pay her tuition and buy new clothes and shoes to wear to class and work? What creative, resourceful ideas (solutions) can you give Jennifer? Study the problem and decide what would be the best action plan. Then recommend three creative solutions for Jennifer.

My creative solutions:

_____

_____

_____

REFLECTIONS
on Critical and Creative Thinking

Thinking critically, solving problems, and making rational decisions require a great deal of commitment on your part. They may not be easy for you at first, but with practice, dedication, and an understanding of the immense need of these skills, you can think more critically, creatively, and logically, evaluate information sources, and use emotional intelligence to your best advantage.

Knowledge
in Bloom

SOLVING A PROBLEM

Each lesson-end assessment is based on Bloom's Taxonomy of Learning. See the first page of this lesson for a quick review.

This activity uses levels 2–6 of the taxonomy

Using the problem-solving diagram in Figure 4.6, the information on problem-solving found in Step Two of this lesson, and the skills you have learned about critical thinking and problem-solving, work through the following scenario and determine the steps to solve this problem. Be certain to identify the **root** of the problem and offer several concrete, realistic solutions.

THE PROBLEM

Your best friend, Nathan, tells you that his parents are really coming down hard on him for going to college. It is a strange problem. They believe that Nathan should be working full time and that he is just wasting his time and money, since he did not do well in high school. They have threatened to take away his car and kick him out of the house if he does not find a full-time job. Nathan is doing well and does not want to leave college. He has a goal of becoming an architect and knows that he has talent in this area. He is making A's and B's in all of his classes. This does not matter to his parents—they do not value education and see it as a luxury.

Figure 4.6 Solutions in Bloom Diagram

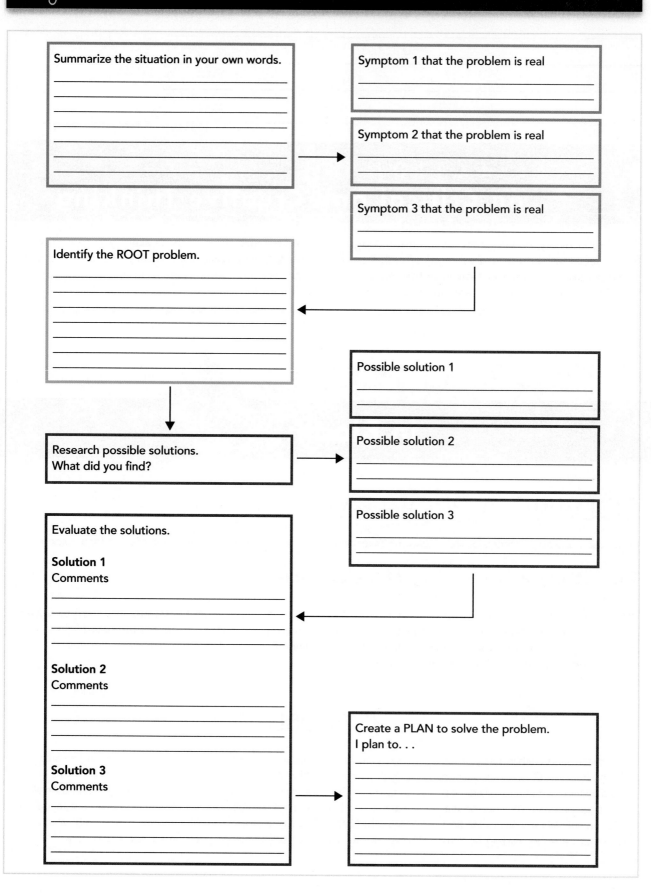

REFERENCES

Goleman, D. (2006). *Emotional Intelligence: Why It Can Matter More Than IQ* (10th Anniversary Edition). New York, NY: Bantam.

MindTools. (2011). The ladder of influence: Avoiding jumping to conclusions. Retrieved May 2, 2011, from www.mindtool.com.

Nelson, D., & Low, G. (2003). *Emotional Intelligence: Achieving Academic and Career Excellence.* Upper Saddle River, NJ: Prentice Hall.

Paul, R., & Elder, L. (2006). *A Miniature Guide to Critical Thinking: Concepts and Tools.* Dillon Beach, CA: Foundation for Critical Thinking.

Snyder, C. R., & Lopez, S. (2007). *Positive Psychology: The Scientific and Practical Explorations of Human Strength.* Thousand Oaks, CA: Sage Publications.

LEARN

DISCOVERING AND APPLYING YOUR LEARNING STYLE

Fotolia

"Only a swimmer knows how swimming feels . . . There is no substitute for experience, none at all."
— Abraham H. Maslow

LEARN

Why read this lesson?

Because you'll learn how to:

- Recommend effective learning strategies for your learning preferences

Because you'll be able to:

- Describe different learning preferences
- Determine your own learning preference
- Recognize classroom and study tactics for different learning preferences

Knowledge in Bloom

Bloom's Taxonomy of Learning is a simple way of explaining the levels at which we all learn material and acquire information. The learning levels progress from basic to more complex learning and thinking. Examples are detailed below. Throughout this lesson, you'll see colorful triangles to the side of some activities. They let you know on which level of Bloom's Taxonomy the questions are based.

- **LEVEL 1: Remember**
  List the three learning styles.

- **LEVEL 2: Understand**
  Explain the learning process.

- **LEVEL 3: Apply**
  Demonstrate how your strengths can be used advantageously.

- **LEVEL 4: Analyze**
  Compare and contrast a learning style and a learning strategy.

- **LEVEL 5: Evaluate**
  Evaluate your learning preference in relation to your study habits and performance.

- **LEVEL 6: Create**
  Propose three strategies for using your learning style to your best advantage.

MyStudentSuccessLab

MyStudentSuccessLab is an online solution designed to help you acquire and develop (or hone) the skills you need to succeed. You will have access to peer-led video presentations and develop core skills through interactive exercises and projects.

THE LEARNING PROCESS

What Are the Steps to Active, Authentic Learning?

Learning can be conscious and/or unconscious. Do you remember the very day you learned how to walk or talk? Probably not. This learning was more of an unconscious nature. However, you probably do remember studying about the fifty states or learning subtraction or reading an Edgar Allen Poe poem for the first time. This learning was more conscious in nature. Learning can also be formal (schooling) or informal ("street knowledge"). Learning can happen in many ways—through play, trial and error, mistakes, successes, repetition, environmental conditioning, parental discipline, social interactions, media, observation, and, yes, through formal study methods.

"Human beings have an innate learning process, which includes a motivation to learn" (Smilkstein, 2003). You may be saying to yourself, *"If I have a natural, innate ability to learn, then why is chemistry so difficult for me to master?" Why is English such a crazy language with so many rules?"* The answer could rest in the notion that you are going ***against*** your natural, neurological learning pattern. That you are being taught, or trying to learn by yourself, in a way that is unnatural to you, and your brain simply is having trouble adapting to this unnatural process.

If you learn best by doing and touching; ***you need to do and touch***. If you learn best by listening and questioning; you need to ***listen and question***. If you learn best by reading and studying in a quiet place; you need to ***find a quiet place to read and study***. Basically, you must figure out your natural inclination for learning and build on it. You will also need to understand that learning takes time, and people need different amounts of time to master material. Janet may learn Concept X in a few hours, but it may take William three days of constant practice to learn the same concept. One thing is true: The more ***involved*** you are with the information you are trying to learn, the more you retain.

In Figure 5.1, we have tried to simplify thousands of years of educational study on the topic of learning. Basically, learning something new can happen in the six steps outlined in Figure 5.1.

GIVE YOUR BRAIN A WORKOUT

Can I Really Learn All of This New Stuff?

Yes! Yes! Yes! You can learn! Think about all that you have already learned in your lifetime. You learned how to eat, walk, talk, play, make decisions, dress yourself, have a conversation, tie your shoes, make your bed, ride a bicycle, play a sport, drive a car, protect yourself, make associations based on observations, use a

Have you encountered people with learning styles different from yours? How?
Fotolia

65

Figure 5.1 The Learning Process

1. Motivation to learn the material is the first step in the learning process. You have to possess the internal motivation and passion to want to learn what is being presented or what you are studying. You must also be motivated enough to devote the time to learning something new. Deep, purposeful learning does not happen in an instant; it takes work, patience, and yes, motivation.

2. Understand the material through ambitious curiosity, keen observations, purposeful questioning, intense studying, eager determination, robust effort, and time devoted to task. You must be able to answer such questions as: Who is involved? What happened? When did it happen? Where did it happen? How did it happen? How could it have happened? What does it all mean? Why is it important? What is the relationship between x and y? You should be able to describe it, discuss it, give examples, put the information into your own words, and tell others about it clearly.

3. Internalize the material by asking, How can this information affect my life, my career, my studies, and my future? Why does this information matter? How can I control my emotions regarding the value of this information? If I think this information is useless, how can I change this perception?

4. Apply the material by asking, How can I use this information to improve? How can I use this information to work with others, to develop new ideas, or to build meaningful conclusions? Can I demonstrate it? Can I share this information with or teach this information to others intelligently? Is it possible to practice what I have learned?

5. Evaluate the material by determining the value of what you just learned. Ask yourself, Do I trust my research and sources? Have I consulted others about their findings and knowledge? What did they learn? What can I learn from them? Have I asked for feedback? Can I debate this information with others?

6. Use the material to grow and change. Ask yourself, How could I take this information (or the process of learning this information) and change my life, attitudes, or emotions? How could this information help me grow? What can I create out of this new information? How can I expand on this knowledge to learn more?

cell phone, play a video game, ask questions, and countless other simple and highly complex skills. There is *proof* that you **can learn** because you **have learned** in the past. The old excuse of *"I can't learn this stuff"* is simply hogwash! You have the capacity to know more, do more, experience more, and acquire more knowledge. Your brain is a natural learning machine just as your heart is a natural pumping machine. It is in our nature to learn every single day. In order to learn new things, however, you have to **devote the time necessary to learn** and then build on that knowledge base.

UNDERSTANDING YOUR STRENGTHS

What Are the Advantages of Discovering and Polishing Innate Talents?

On the next few pages, you will have the opportunity to complete an inventory to identify your learning style. At the end of the lesson, you will have the opportunity to pull all of this information together to help you understand your learning preferences and to formulate a learning plan for the future.

This assessment is in no way intended to "label you." It is not a measure of how smart you are. It does not measure your worth or your capacities as a student. This assessment is included so that you might gain a better understanding of your learning style and preferences for how you learn.

There are no right or wrong answers and there is not one "*best way*" to learn. We hope that by the end of this lesson, you will have experienced a "Wow" or an "Ah-ha!" moment as you explore and discover new and exciting things about you and your education. We also hope that by the end of this lesson, you will have the skills needed to more effectively use your dominant traits and improve your less dominant characteristics.

KNOWING THE *HOW* IS *HALF* THE BATTLE

What Is Your Learning Preference?

A learning preference is "*the way in which each learner begins to concentrate on, process, and retain new and difficult information*" (Dunn & Griggs, 2000). There is a difference between a *learning preference* and a *learning strategy*. A learning *preference* is innate and involves your five senses. It is how you best process information that comes to you. A learning *strategy* is how you might choose to learn or study, such as by using notecards, flip charts, color slides, or cooperative learning groups. Learning strategies also involve where you study (such as at a desk, in bed, in the library, in a quiet place, with music, etc.), how long you study, and what techniques you use to help you study (such as mnemonics, cooperative learning teams, or SQ3R).

> "Education is learning what you did not know you did not know."
> —Daniel Boorstin

If you learn best by *seeing* information, you have a more dominant **visual learning style**. If you learn best by *hearing* information, you have a more dominant **auditory learning style**. If you learn best by *touching or doing,* you have a more dominant **tactile learning style**. You may also hear the tactile learning style referred to as kinesthetic or hands-on.

Some of the most successful students master information and techniques by using all three styles. If you were learning how to skateboard, you might learn best by **hearing someone** talk about the different styles or techniques. Others might learn best by **watching a video** where someone demonstrates the techniques. Still others would learn best by actually getting on the board and **trying it.** Those who engage all of their senses gain the most.

from **ordinary** to Extraordinary

Sylvia Eberhardt, Fashion Model, Abercrombie and Fitch and Hollister Magazine

If you read Sylvia's resume and professional credits, you might think she had it made—that the world had been handed to her on a silver platter. Nothing could be further from the truth. Although she is an honors student at Howard University and a fashion model having worked with some of the top stores and magazines in the nation, her beginnings were anything but easy and beautiful.

Sylvia was born into a crack-infested, gang-ridden, one bedroom house in inner city Washington, DC. She was raised a few doors down from a major crack house where she saw junkies, prostitutes, and pimps on a daily basis. Poverty surrounded Sylvia and her two siblings at every turn. She slept in a bunk bed where nightly she could hear drug deals being made outside her window. The iron bars on her windows were the only thing that separated her from the ugliness of the world outside her home.

Sylvia's mother died just before she entered high school and she was raised from that point on by her father. She was constantly teased and tormented growing up because she was so thin. Her peers nicknamed her Anna (for anorexic). What her

DIFFERENT STROKES FOR DIFFERENT FOLKS

Do Study Tactics Really Vary from Person to Person and Class to Class?

Just as few people see every issue the same way, few people learn and study the same. For some people, they may study well in groups, talking with each other with music playing. For others, they must study alone in total silence. In the classroom, some people may love to work in groups, while others prefer that the instructor lecture with outline notes and visuals. If you find that your primary learning preference is visual and you take a class that is totally lecture (oral), don't automatically think that you're going to fail. You can overcome this obstacle with work and planning. The trick to making your learning preference work for you is to figure out exactly what tactics work best for you and how to use them to best advantage. Remember, your study tactics may change from class to class.

Let's say that you are taking an English class and your instructor does nothing but lecture. You have very little chance to "do" anything, "see" anything, or "say" anything in class. You get to listen. You have discovered that your primary learning preference is visual—meaning that you learn best by seeing things in charts, graphs, pictures, etc. Is all lost? Not at all. Before and after class you will need to do some prep work to help you *during* class. For example, if you know that your instructor is going to lecture on writing effective paragraphs, you will certainly want to read the section in the book (which engages your visual learning

peers did not know was that Sylvia suffered (and continues to suffer) from Crohn's disease, a life-threatening, autoimmune disease affecting the gastro-intestinal system, causing rashes, severe abdominal pain, arthritis, vomiting, and weight loss.

How did she survive and thrive? She was blessed to have an amazing, supportive father who taught her that you never have to let your past or present dictate your future. Her father taught her that no matter how humble her beginnings might have been, no matter where she was born or the circumstances of her life, the test of her character would be knowing that she held her destiny in her own hands. He often said to Sylvia and her siblings, "You may live in the ghetto, but the ghetto does not have to live in you."

> Her father taught her, "You may live in the ghetto, but the ghetto does not have to live in you."

After moving to Virginia, she began working hard and taking college-level classes at Northern Virginia Community College, dreaming of becoming a heart surgeon. By the end of her second term she had a 4.0 GPA. She won a full scholarship to Howard University. She changed her life from ordinary to extraordinary!

EXTRAORDINARY REFLECTION

Sylvia's father said to her, "you may live in the ghetto, but the ghetto does not have to live in you." How do you plan to use your past experiences, positive or negative, or the advice of others, to bring about positive change in your future?

preference to a certain degree), but you may also want to go online and do a search for a video on writing effective paragraphs. Watch the video and practice writing a paragraph (this engages your visual and tactile learning preferences). Then, when you get to class, you have prepared to *hear* the lecture and you can make mental notes based on the video you watched and the sample paragraph you prepared. This is an example of how you can create learning plans and study tactics to enhance your learning preference. This technique may change from class to class.

In the Knowledge in Bloom activity at the end of this lesson you will have the opportunity to create learning paths and study tactics for each learning preference. Take a moment now and complete the LEAD in Figure 5.2 on page 70. This assessment will help you determine your learning preference.

REFLECTIONS
on Learning How to Learn

Discovering your learning preference can greatly enhance your classroom performance. For example, finally understanding that your learning preference is visual and that your professor's teaching preference is totally verbal (oral) can answer many questions about why you may have performed poorly in the past in a strictly "lecture class" or wonderfully in a class where many visuals are used. It is paramount to your success to use this knowledge and develop tools to make your learning preference work for you, not against you.

Figure 5.2 Take the LEAD (Learning Evaluation and Assessment Directory)

Directions: Read each statement carefully and thoroughly. After reading the statement, rate your response using the scale below. There are no right or wrong answers. This is not a timed survey. The LEAD is based, in part, on research conducted by Rita Dunn.

3 = Often Applies

2 = Sometimes Applies

1 = Never or Almost Never Applies

_____ 1. I remember information better if I write it down or draw a picture of it.

_____ 2. I remember things better when I hear them instead of just reading or seeing them.

_____ 3. When I get something that has to be assembled, I just start doing it. I don't read the directions.

_____ 4. If I am taking a test, I can "see" the page of the text or lecture notes where the answer is located.

_____ 5. I would rather the professor explain a graph, chart, or diagram than just show it to me.

_____ 6. When learning new things, I want to "do it" rather than hear about it.

_____ 7. I would rather the instructor write the information on the board, use a Power-Point, or show a video instead of just lecturing.

_____ 8. I would rather listen to a book on tape than read it.

_____ 9. I enjoy making things, putting things together, and working with my hands.

_____ 10. I am able to quickly conceptualize and visualize information.

_____ 11. I learn best by hearing words.

_____ 12. I have been called "hyperactive" by my parents, spouse, partner, or professor.

_____ 13. I have no trouble reading maps, charts, and diagrams.

_____ 14. I can usually pick up on small sounds like bells, crickets, and frogs, and distant sounds like train whistles.

_____ 15. I use my hands and gesture a lot when I speak to others.

Refer to your score on each individual question. Place that score beside the appropriate question number below. Then, tally the total for each line at the side.

SCORE					TOTAL ACROSS	CODE
1 ___	4 ___	7 ___	10 ___	13 ___	___	Visual
2 ___	5 ___	8 ___	11 ___	14 ___	___	Auditory
3 ___	6 ___	9 ___	12 ___	15 ___	___	Tactile

© Robert M. Sherfield

in Bloom

USING YOUR LEARNING PREFERENCE TO CREATE YOUR LEARNING AND STUDY PLAN

Each lesson-end assessment is based on Bloom's Taxonomy of Learning. See the first page of this lesson for a quick review.

This activity uses levels 2–6 of the taxonomy

Visual Learning Preference (Eye Smart) Thinks in pictures; enjoys visual instructions, demonstrations, and descriptions; would rather read a text than listen to a lecture; avid note-taker; needs visual references; enjoys using charts, graphs, and pictures.	I can use my visual learning preference to enhance my learning plan and study tactics by . . . 1. _____ 2. _____ 3. _____	I can use my visual learning preference to prepare for exams by . . . 1. _____ 2. _____ 3. _____
Auditory Learning Preference (Ear Smart) Prefers verbal instructions; would rather listen than read; often tapes lectures and listens to them in the car or at home; recites information out loud; enjoys talking, discussing issues, and verbal stimuli; talks out problems.	I can use my auditory learning preference to enhance my learning plan and study tactics by . . . 1. _____ 2. _____ 3. _____	I can use my auditory learning preference to prepare for exams by . . . 1. _____ 2. _____ 3. _____
Tactile Learning Preference (Action Smart) Prefers hands-on approaches to learning; likes to take notes and uses a great deal of scratch paper; learns best by doing something, by touching it, or manipulating it; learns best while moving or while in action; often does not concentrate well when sitting still and reading.	I can use my tactile learning preference to enhance my learning plan and study tactics by . . . 1. _____ 2. _____ 3. _____	I can use my tactile learning preference to prepare for exams by . . . 1. _____ 2. _____ 3. _____

REFERENCES

Dunn, R., & Griggs, S. (2000). *Practical Approaches to Using Learning Styles in Higher Education.* New York, NY: Bergin & Garvey.

Smilkstein, R. (2003). *We're Born to Learn: Using the Brain's Natural Learning Process to Create Today's Curriculum.* Thousand Oaks, CA: Corwin Press.

RECORD

CULTIVATING YOUR LISTENING SKILLS AND FINDING A NOTE-TAKING SYSTEM THAT WORKS FOR YOU

"To listen well is as powerful a means of communication as to talk well." —Chinese Proverb

RECORD

Why read this lesson?

Because you'll learn how to:

- Create class notes using active listening techniques

Because you'll be able to:

- Describe how to prepare for class
- Explain techniques for active listening
- Analyze characteristics of effective in-class notes
- Compare different in-class note-taking strategies.

Knowledge in Bloom

Bloom's Taxonomy of Learning is a simple way of explaining the levels at which we all learn material and acquire information. The learning levels progress from basic to more complex learning and thinking. Examples are detailed below. Throughout this lesson, you'll see colorful triangles to the side of some activities. They let you know on which level of Bloom's Taxonomy the questions are based.

- **LEVEL 1: Remember**
  Describe the difference between listening and hearing.
- **LEVEL 2: Understand**
  Summarize the four listening styles.
- **LEVEL 3: Apply**
  Demonstrate techniques of active listening.
- **LEVEL 4: Analyze**
  Compare and contrast two note-taking styles.
- **LEVEL 5: Evaluate**
  Recommend a note-taking style for math.
- **LEVEL 6: Create**
  Write notes for one class using the Cornell method.

MyStudentSuccessLab

MyStudentSuccessLab is an online solution designed to help you acquire and develop (or hone) the skills you need to succeed. You will have access to peer-led video presentations and develop core skills through interactive exercises and projects.

THE IMPORTANCE OF LISTENING

Why Does Listening Really Matter in Classes and Relationships?

Listening is a survival skill. Period! It is that simple! *"I know listening is important,"* you might say, but few ever think of the paramount significance listening has on our everyday lives. It is necessary for:

- Establishing and improving relationships
- Personal growth
- Showing respect to others
- Professional rapport
- Showing empathy and compassion
- Learning new information
- Understanding others' opinions and views
- Basic survival
- Entertainment
- Health

How can becoming a critical listener help you in and out of the classroom?
Shutterstock

How much time do you think you spend listening every day? Research suggests that we spend almost 70 percent of our waking time communicating, and **53 percent of that time is spent in listening situations** (Adler, Rosenfeld, & Proctor, 2010). Effective listening skills can mean the difference between success or failure, A's or F's, relationships or loneliness, and in some cases and careers, life or death.

For students, good listening skills are critical. Over the next two to four years, you will be given a lot of information through lectures. Cultivating and improving your active listening skills will help you prepare for your classes, understand the material, take accurate notes, participate in class discussions, communicate with your peers more effectively, and become more actively engaged in your learning process.

I THINK I HEARD YOU LISTENING

Is There Really a Difference between Listening and Hearing?

No doubt you've been in a communication situation where a misunderstanding took place. Either you hear something incorrectly or someone hears you incorrectly *or* it could be that someone hears your message but misinterprets it. These communication blunders arise because we tend to view listening (and communication in general) as an automatic response when in fact it is not.

"You cannot truly listen to anyone and do anything else at the same time."
—M. Scott Peck

Listening is a learned, voluntary activity. You must choose to do it. It is a skill just as driving a car, painting a picture, or playing the piano. Becoming an active listener requires practice, time, mistakes, guidance, and active participation.

Hearing, however, is not learned; it is automatic and involuntary. Unless you have a physical condition, if you are within range of a sound you will probably hear it although you may not be listening to it. Hearing a sound does not guarantee that you know from where it comes and who/what made the sound. Listening actively, though, means making a conscious effort to focus on the sound you heard and to determine what it is.

LISTENING DEFINED

Is Listening with the Heart Possible?

According to Ronald Adler (Adler, Rosenfeld, & Proctor, 2010), the drawing of the Chinese verb "to listen" (Figure 6.1) provides a comprehensive and practical definition of listening.

To the Chinese, listening involves the ***ears***, the ***eyes***, your ***undivided attention***, and the ***heart***. Do you make it a habit to listen with more than your ears? The Chinese view listening as a whole-body experience. People from Western cultures seem to have lost the ability to involve their whole body in the listening process. We tend to use only our ears, and sometimes we don't even use them very well.

At its core, listening is "the ability to hear, understand, analyze, respect, and appropriately respond to the meaning of another person's spoken and nonverbal messages" (Daly & Engleberg, 2006). Although this definition involves the word "hear," listening goes far beyond just the physical ability to catch sound waves.

The first step in listening *is* hearing, but true listening involves one's full attention and the ability to filter out distractions, emotional barriers, cultural differences, and religious biases. Listening means that you are making a conscious decision to understand and show reverence for the other person's communication efforts.

Figure 6.1 Chinese Verb, "To Listen"

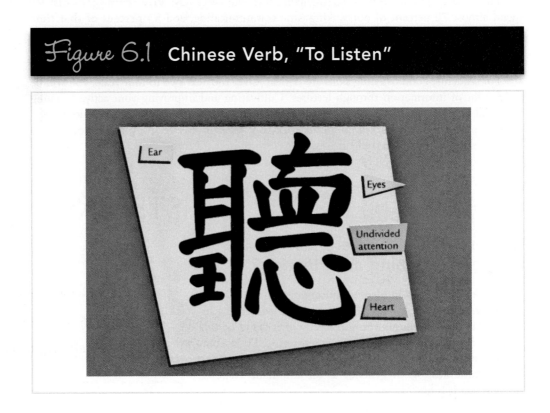

from ordinary to

Extraordinary

Dino J. Gonzalez, M.D., Internal Medical Associates, Las Vegas, NV, Board-Certified Internal Medicine and AAHIVM Certified HIV Specialist

Can one person make a difference in your life? Can one person change the course of your destiny? The answer is yes! Most definitely, yes! The person who altered the course of Dr. Gonzalez's future was his third-grade teacher, Mrs. Allison. She was a strong African American lady who pushed her class to do their best. She was hard and demanded the best from the class, but she was fair and an awesome teacher. She corrected their grammar and let them know that "street English" would not fly in her classroom. She even made her classes do Jazzercise after lunch to teach them how to take care of their bodies.

> Dr. Gonzalez was born in a HUD housing project in a gang-infested area of Las Vegas, Nevada.

Why was she so dynamic? Why did she mean so much to Dr. Gonzalez? Well, he had always been a good student in school, earning mostly A's. However, his home life was another story. He was born in 1970 in a HUD housing project in Las Vegas, Nevada, in the gang-infested 28th Street area. His mother, two brothers, and he lived in poverty. By the time he was three, his mother was bedridden and on disability due to chronic obstructive pulmonary disease, caused by a three-pack-a-day smoking habit. The family was on welfare, food stamps, and the free lunch program.

As it turned out, his father never married his mother or helped support the children because he was already married to another woman with children of their own. Dr. Gonzalez's mother did not know this until after his birth. They were on their own. Often, Dr. Gonzalez felt alone in his community because he looked different. His father was Latino, but his mother was a blond, light-skinned Norwegian. He was not brown. He was not white. He felt like he did not have a real place in the community or in school. Mrs. Allison helped change all of that for Dr. Gonzalez. Because of Mrs. Allison's influence, he began to surround himself with people who were positive and worked hard. He wanted to be around people who *wanted something*—who had a more visionary view of the world than he had.

He had always loved science and the study of the human body, so he decided to major in chemistry and education. He began to develop a keen interest in infectious diseases and viruses. By the time he was a junior in college, he had decided to become a doctor. After graduation, he applied to medical school and was accepted into the University of Nevada School of Medicine. He completed his studies, did a three-year residency, and became board certified in internal medicine as an HIV specialist. His dream of doing something real and helping others is now an everyday occurrence in his life. He moved from ordinary to extraordinary.

EXTRAORDINARY REFLECTION

Dr. Gonzalez talks about his teacher, Mrs. Allison, and how she challenged him and changed his life. What teacher has dramatically altered the course of your life? How?

FOUR LISTENING STYLES DEFINED

What Is Your Orientation?

According to Steven McCornack (2007), interpersonal communication expert, author, and educator, there are *four different listening styles*. **They are action-oriented, time-oriented, people-oriented, and content-oriented.** Study Figure 6.2 to determine which best describes you as a listener.

Figure 6.2 Four Listening Styles

Action-Oriented Listeners

- Want to get their messages quickly and to-the-point
- Do not like fluff and grow impatient when they perceive people to be wasting their time
- Become frustrated when information is not orderly
- Are quick to dismiss people who ramble and falter when they speak.

Time-Oriented Listeners

- Want their information in brief, concise messages
- Are consumed with how much time is taken to convey a message
- Set time limits for listening (and communicating in general)
- Will ask people to "move the message along" if they feel it is taking too long

People-Oriented Listeners

- Are in contrast to time- and action-oriented listeners
- View listening as a chance to connect with other people
- Enjoy listening to people so that relationships can be built
- Become emotionally involved with the person communicating

Content-Oriented Listeners

- Enjoy an intellectual challenge
- Like to listen to technical information, facts, and evidence
- Enjoy complex information that must be deciphered and filtered
- Carefully evaluate information and facts before forming an opinion
- Enjoy asking questions

Which style best describes you? _____

What are the "pros" of being this type of listener? _____

_____

_____

_____

What are the "cons" of being this type of listener?_____

_____

_____

_____

MASTERING THE TECHNIQUES OF ACTIVE LISTENING

Can You Really Overcome the Obstacles to Listening?

Several major obstacles stand in the way of becoming an effective, active listener. To begin building active listening skills, you first have to remove some barriers.

Obstacle One: Prejudging

Prejudging means that you automatically shut out what is being said, one of the biggest obstacles to active listening. You may prejudge because you don't like or agree with the information or the person communicating. You may also have prejudging problems because of your environment, culture, social status, or attitude.

TIPS FOR OVERCOMING PREJUDGING

- Listen for information that may be valuable to you as a student. Some material may not be pleasant to hear but may be useful to you later on.
- Listen to the message, not the messenger. If you do not like the speaker, try to go beyond personality and listen to what is being said, without regard to the person saying it. Conversely, you may like the speaker so much that you automatically accept the material or answers without listening objectively to what is being said.
- Try to remove cultural, racial, gender, social, and environmental barriers. Just because a person is different from you or holds a different point of view does not make that person wrong; and just because a person is like you and holds a similar point of view does not make that person right. Sometimes, you have to cross cultural and environmental barriers to learn new material and see with brighter eyes.

Obstacle Two: Talking

Not even the best listener in the world can listen while he or she is talking. The next time you are in a conversation with a friend, try speaking while your friend is speaking—then see if you know what your friend said. To become an effective listener, you need to learn the power of silence. Silence gives you the opportunity to think about what is being said before you respond. The first rule of listening is: stop talking. The second rule of listening is: stop talking. And you guessed it—the third rule of listening is stop talking.

TIPS FOR OVERCOMING THE URGE TO TALK TOO MUCH

- Avoid interrupting the speaker. Force yourself to be silent at parties, family gatherings, and friendly get-togethers. You should not be unsociable, but force yourself to be silent for 10 minutes. You'll be surprised at what you hear. You may also be surprised how hard it is to do this. Test yourself.

■ Ask someone a question and then allow that person to answer the question.

■ Too often we ask questions and answer them ourselves. Force yourself to wait until the person has formulated a response. If you ask questions and wait for answers, you will force yourself to listen.

■ Concentrate on what is being said at the moment, not what you want to say next.

Do you find it easy or hard to pick up the clues a professor gives in class that may indicate important test information?
iStockPhoto

Obstacle Three: Becoming Too Emotional

Emotions can form a strong barrier to active listening. Worries, problems, fears, and anger can keep you from listening to the greatest advantage. Have you ever sat in a lecture, and before you knew what was happening, your mind was a million miles away because you were angry or worried about something? If you have, you know what it's like to bring your emotions to the table.

TIPS FOR OVERCOMING EMOTIONS

■ Know how you feel before you begin the listening experience. Take stock of your emotions and feelings ahead of time.

■ Focus on the message; determine how to use the information.

■ Create a positive image about the message you are hearing.

■ Avoid overreacting and jumping to conclusions.

LISTENING FOR KEY WORDS, PHRASES, AND HINTS

Can Key Words Be Identified to Study Material and Prepare for Class?

Learning how to listen for key words, phrases, and hints can help you become an active listener and an effective note taker, thus helping you prepare for the information you'll hear in class. For example, if your English instructor begins a lecture saying, "*There are ten basic elements to writing poetry,*" jot down the number 10 under the heading "Poetry," or number your notebook page 1 through 10, leaving space for notes. If at the end of class you listed six elements to writing poetry, you know that you missed a part of the lecture. At this point, you need to ask the instructor some questions.

Here are some key phrases and words to listen for:

in addition to	another way	above all
most important	such as	specifically
you'll see this again	therefore	finally
for example	to illustrate	as stated earlier
in contrast	in comparison	nevertheless
the characteristics of	the main issue is	moreover
on the other hand	as a result of	because

Picking up on *transition words* such as these will help you filter out less important information and thus listen more carefully to what is most important. There are other indicators of important information as well that will help you succeed in class. You will want to listen carefully when the instructor:

- Writes something on the board
- Uses a PowerPoint or Prezi presentation
- Uses computer-aided graphics
- Speaks in a louder tone or changes vocal patterns
- Uses gestures more than usual
- Draws on a flip chart

TAKING EFFECTIVE NOTES

Is It Just a Big, Crazy Chore?

Go to class, listen, and write it down. Read a text, take notes. Watch a film, take notes. Is it really that important? Actually, knowing how to take useful, accurate notes can dramatically improve your life as a student. If you are an effective listener and note taker, you have two of the most valuable skills any student could ever use. There are several reasons why it is important to take notes:

- You become an active part of the listening process.
- You create a history of your course content when you take notes.
- You have written criteria to follow when studying.
- You create a visual aid for your material.
- Studying becomes much easier.
- You retain information at a greater rate than non-note takers.
- Effective note takers average higher grades than non-note takers (Kiewra & Fletcher, 1984).

COMPARING THE CHARACTERISTICS OF EFFECTIVE IN-CLASS NOTES

What Are the Steps to Active Preparation for Class?

You have already learned several skills you will need to take notes, such as cultivating your active listening skills, overcoming obstacles to effective listening, and familiarizing yourself with key phrases used by instructors. Next, prepare yourself mentally and physically to take effective notes that are going to be helpful to you. Consider the following ideas as you think about expanding your note-taking abilities.

- **Physically and mentally "attend class."** This refers to the classroom and online instruction. This may sound like stating the obvious, but it is surprising how many students feel they do not need to do anything to learn.
- Come to **class prepared**. Scan, read, and use your textbook to establish a basic understanding of the material **before** coming to class. It is always easier to take notes when you have a preliminary understanding of what is being said. Coming to class prepared also means bringing the proper materials for taking notes: lab manuals, pens,

How can good note taking skills help you gather and retain information?
Shutterstock

a notebook, a highlighter, perhaps your computer.

■ **Bring your textbook** to class. Although many students think they do not need to bring their textbooks to class if they have read the homework, you will find that many instructors repeatedly refer to the text while lecturing. The instructor may ask you to highlight, underline, or refer to the text in class, and following along in the text as the instructor lectures may also help you organize your notes.

■ **Ask questions** and participate in class. Two of the most critical actions you can perform in class are to ask questions and to participate in the class discussion. If you do not understand a concept or theory, ask questions. Don't leave class without understanding what has happened and assume you'll pick it up on your own.

COMPARING THE THREE COMMON NOTE-TAKING SYSTEMS

Why Doesn't Everyone Listen and Take Notes the Same Way?

There are three common note-taking systems: (1) the *outline* technique; (2) the **Cornell**, or split-page technique (also called the T system); and (3) the *mapping* technique. You will find that you may have to use a combination of all three to capture the notes from lectures, readings, and online instruction. You may prefer the Cornell method, but in some instances, the outline technique may serve you better. The following section will give you descriptions and examples of each. Do not feel that you must choose one—try them all and see what works best for you in each situation.

IT'S AS SIMPLE AS A, B, C—1, 2, 3

The Outline Technique

The outline system uses a series of major headings and multiple subheadings formatted in hierarchical order (see Figure 6.3). The outline technique is one of the most commonly used note-taking systems, yet it is also one of the most misused systems. It can be difficult to outline notes in class, especially if your instructor does not follow an outline while lecturing.

When using the outline system, it is best to get all the information from the lecture, and then afterward to combine your lecture notes and text notes to create an outline. Most instructors

Figure 6.3   The Outline Technique

October 20

Topic: Maslow's Hierarchy of Basic Needs

I. Abraham Maslow (1908–1970)
 – American psychologist
 – Born - Raised Brooklyn, N.Y.
 – Parents = Uneducated Jewish immigrants
 – Lonely - unhappy childhood
 – 1st studied law @ city coll. of N.Y.
 – Grad school - Univ of Wisconsin
 – Studied human behavior & experience
 – Leader of humanistic school of psy.

II. H of B. Needs (Theory)
 – Written in <u>A Theory of Human Motivation</u> in 1943
 – Needs of human arranged like a ladder
 – Basic needs of food, air, water at bottom
 – Higher needs "up" the ladder
 – Lower needs must be met to experience the higher needs

III. H of B. Needs (Features)
 – Physiological needs
  – Breathing
  – Food
  – Air & water
  – Sleep
 – Safety needs
  – Security of body
  – Employment

would advise against using the outline system of note taking in class, although you may be able to use a modified version. The most important thing to remember is not to get bogged down in a system during class; what is critical is getting the ideas down on paper. You can always go back after class and rearrange your notes as needed.

If you are going to use a modified or informal outline while taking notes in class, you may want to consider grouping information together under a heading as a means of outlining. It is easier to remember information that is logically grouped than to remember information that is scattered across several pages. If your study skills lecture is on listening, you might outline your notes using the headings "The Process of Listening" and "Definitions of Listening."

After you have rewritten your notes using class lecture information and material from your textbook, your notes may look like those in Figure 6.3.

IT'S A SPLIT DECISION

The Cornell (Modified Cornell, Split Page, or T) System

The basic principle of the Cornell system, developed by Dr. Walter Pauk of Cornell University, is to split the page into two sections, each section to be used for different information. Section A is used for questions that summarize information found in Section B; Section B is used for the actual notes from class. The blank note-taking page may look like Figure 6.4.

Figure 6.4 **Blank Cornell Frame**

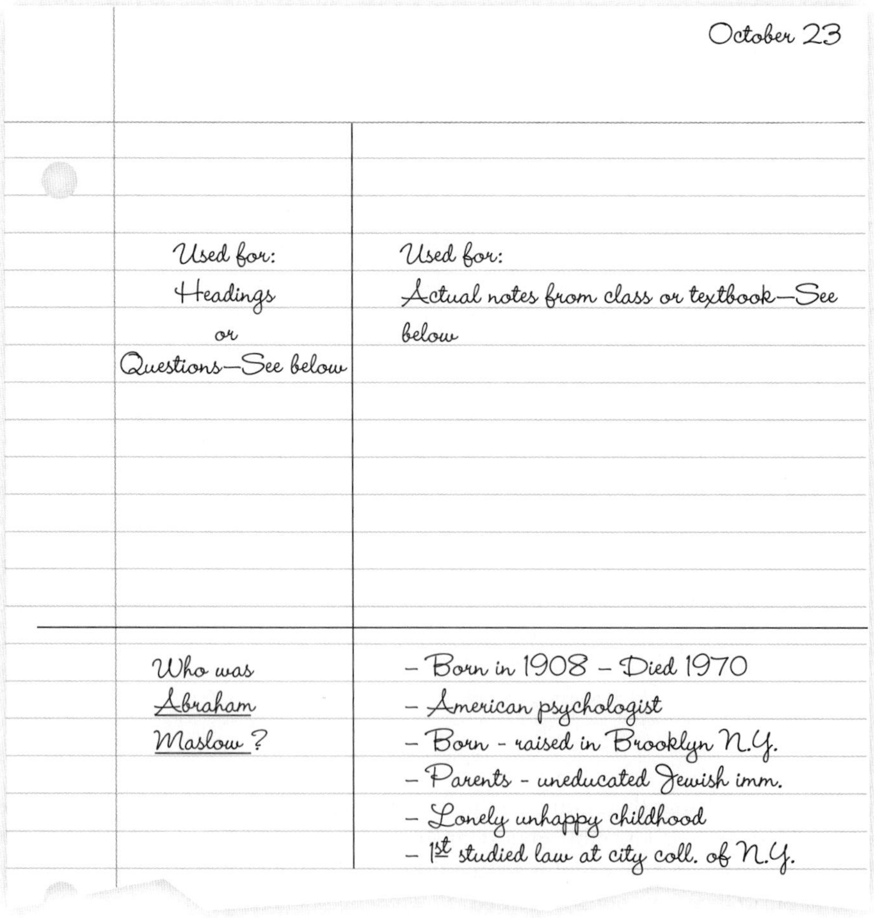

October 23

Used for:
Headings
or
Questions—See below

Used for:
Actual notes from class or textbook—See below

Who was
Abraham
Maslow ?

– Born in 1908 – Died 1970
– American psychologist
– Born - raised in Brooklyn N.Y.
– Parents - uneducated Jewish imm.
– Lonely unhappy childhood
– 1st studied law at city coll. of N.Y.

To implement the Cornell system, you will want to choose the technique that is most comfortable and beneficial for you; you might use mapping (discussed below) or outlining on a Cornell page. An example of *outline notes* using the Cornell system appears in Figure 6.5.

Figure 6.5   The Outline System in a Cornell Frame

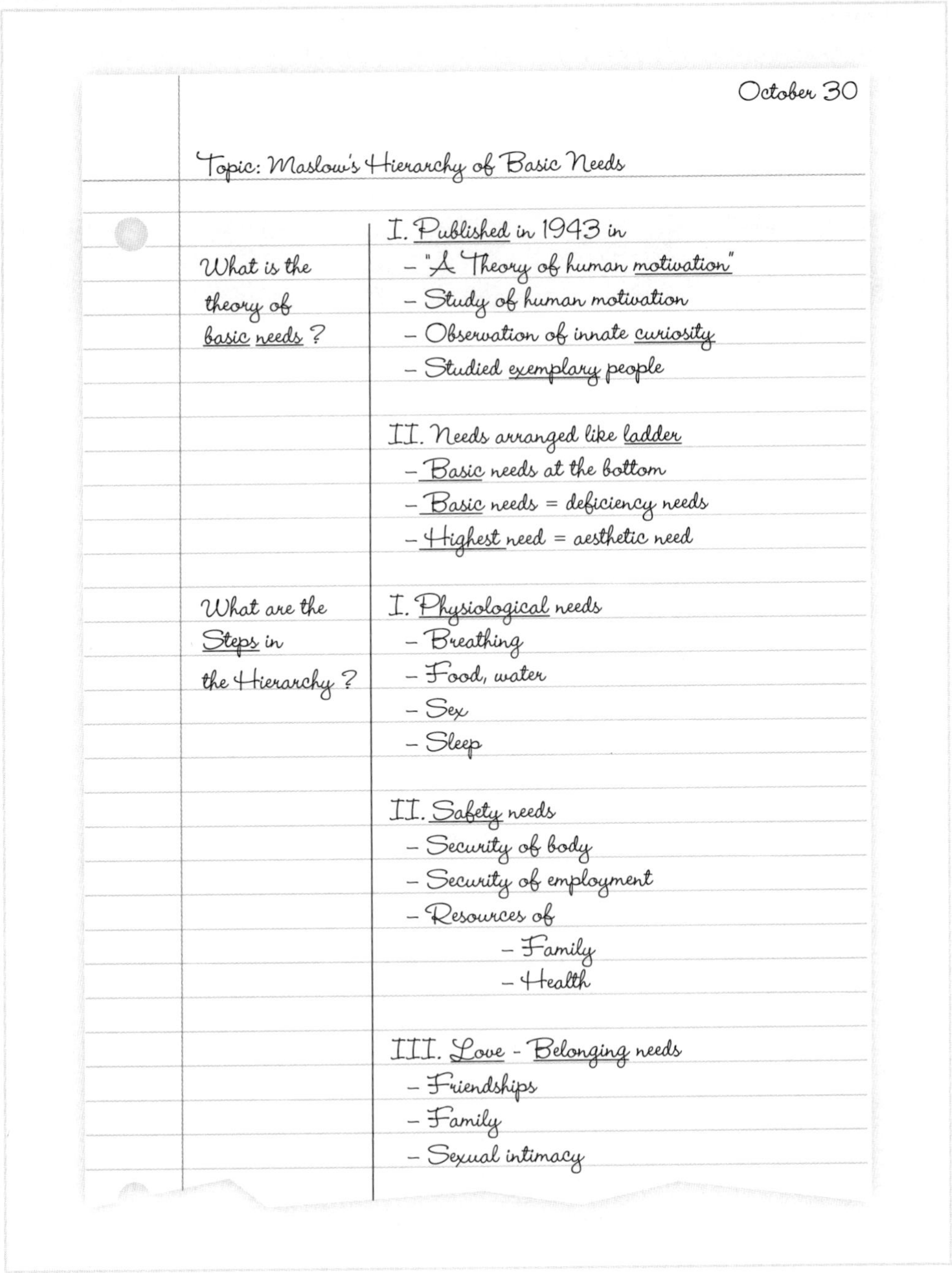

October 30

Topic: Maslow's Hierarchy of Basic Needs

What is the theory of basic needs?	I. Published in 1943 in
	  – "A Theory of human motivation"
	  – Study of human motivation
	  – Observation of innate curiosity
	  – Studied exemplary people
	
	II. Needs arranged like ladder
	  – Basic needs at the bottom
	  – Basic needs = deficiency needs
	  – Highest need = aesthetic need

What are the Steps in the Hierarchy?	I. Physiological needs
	  – Breathing
	  – Food, water
	  – Sex
	  – Sleep
	
	II. Safety needs
	  – Security of body
	  – Security of employment
	  – Resources of
	      – Family
	      – Health
	
	III. Love - Belonging needs
	  – Friendships
	  – Family
	  – Sexual intimacy

GOING AROUND IN CIRCLES

The Mapping System

If you are a visual learner, the mapping system may be especially useful for you. The mapping system of note taking generates a picture of information (see Figure 6.6). The mapping system creates a map, or web, of information that allows you to see the relationships among facts or ideas. A mapping system using a Cornell frame might look something like the notes in Figure 6.7.

The most important thing to remember about each note-taking system is that ***it must work for you***. Do not use a system because your friends use it or because you feel that you should use it. Experiment with each system or combination to determine which is best for you.

Always remember to keep your notes organized, dated, and neat. Notes that cannot be read are no good to you or to anyone else.

Figure 6.6　**The Mapping System**

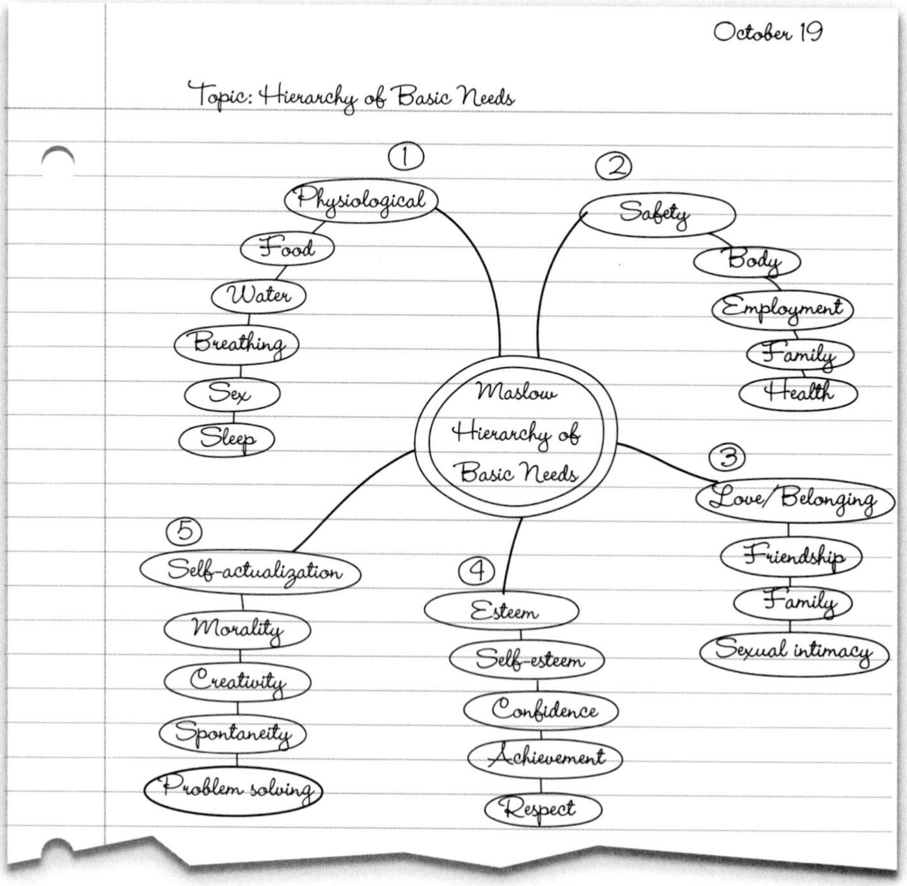

Figure 6.7 The Mapping System in a Cornell Frame

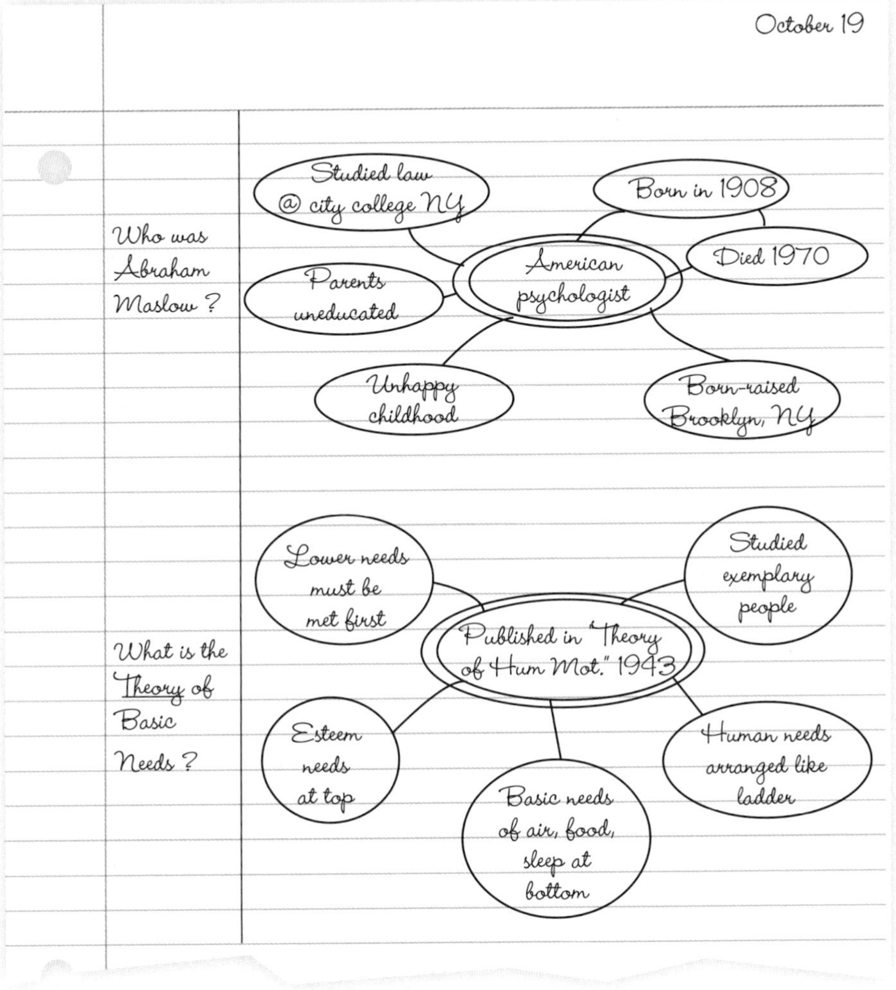

October 19

Who was Abraham Maslow?

- Studied law @ city college NY
- Born in 1908
- Parents uneducated
- American psychologist
- Died 1970
- Unhappy childhood
- Born-raised Brooklyn, NY

What is the Theory of Basic Needs?

- Lower needs must be met first
- Studied exemplary people
- Published in "Theory of Hum Mot." 1943
- Esteem needs at top
- Human needs arranged like ladder
- Basic needs of air, food, sleep at bottom

REFLECTIONS
on Listening and Note Taking

Yes, listening is a learned skill, but it is more than that. It is a gift that you give to yourself. It is a gift that promotes knowledge, understanding, stronger relationships, and open-mindedness. Good listening skills can help you manage conflict, avoid misunderstandings, and establish trusting relationships. Perhaps most importantly at this point in your life, listening can help you become a more successful student. Once you learn how to listen with your whole body and mind, you will begin to see how your notes, your grades, your attitude, your relationships, and your learning processes change.

Knowledge
in Bloom

EVALUATING YOUR NOTE-TAKING SYSTEM

Each lesson-end assessment is based on Bloom's Taxonomy of Learning. See the first page of this lesson for a quick review.

This activity uses levels 3–6 of the taxonomy

Consider the classes for which you are registered this term. Select at least two of them. If you are only taking one class, consider a class that you will be required to take in the future. In the chart below, determine which note taking system would work best for you in this class based on the information and examples in this lesson. Justify why you chose this system. Show an example for each class.

CLASS	SELECTED NOTE TAKING SYSTEM	JUSTIFICATION
1.		

Show an example.

CLASS	SELECTED NOTE TAKING SYSTEM	JUSTIFICATION
2.		

Show an example.

REFERENCES

Adler, R., Rosenfeld, L., & Proctor, R. (2009). *Interplay: The Process of Interpersonal Communication*. New York, NY: Oxford University Press.

Adler, R., Rosenfeld, L., and Proctor, R. (2010). *Interplay: The Process of Interpersonal Communication* (11th ed.). New York, NY: Oxford University Press.

Daly, J., & Engleberg, I. (2006). *Presentations in Everyday Life: Strategies for Effective Speaking*. Upper Saddle River, NJ: Allyn and Bacon.

Kiewra, K., & Fletcher, H. (1984). The relationship between note taking variables and achievement measures. *Human Learning*, 3, 273–280.

McCornack, S. (2007). *Reflect and Relate: An Introduction to Interpersonal Communication*. Boston: Bedford-St. Martin's Press.

READ

BUILDING YOUR READING
AND COMPREHENSION SKILLS

"The difference between the right word and the almost right word is the difference between lightning and the lightning bug." —Mark Twain

READ

Why read this lesson?

Because you'll learn how to:

- Create reading notes using active reading techniques

Because you'll be able to:

- Explain the process of active reading
- Discover your reading style
- Describe highlighting and annotating techniques
- Explain different strategies for taking notes from reading materials
- Combine class and text notes

Knowledge in Bloom

Bloom's Taxonomy of Learning is a simple way of explaining the levels at which we all learn material and acquire information. The learning levels progress from basic to more complex learning and thinking. Examples are detailed below. Throughout this lesson, you'll see colorful triangles to the side of some activities. They let you know on which level of Bloom's Taxonomy the questions are based.

- **LEVEL 1: Remember**
  Describe your reading style.
- **LEVEL 2: Understand**
  Discuss fixation.
- **LEVEL 3: Apply**
  Demonstrate how your attitude affects reading skills.
- **LEVEL 4: Analyze**
  Test your reading comprehension.
- **LEVEL 5: Evaluate**
  Evaluate the SQ3R system of note taking.
- **LEVEL 6: Create**
  Create a succinct synopsis of an article.

MyStudentSuccessLab

MyStudentSuccessLab is an online solution designed to help you acquire and develop (or hone) the skills you need to succeed. You will have access to peer-led video presentations and develop core skills through interactive exercises and projects.

GETTING READY TO READ COLLEGE-LEVEL MATERIAL

Is Reading Fundamental or Just Pure Torture?

Quick question: What are the top two academic problems among students today? According to faculty members, assessments, national tests, and, yes, even your peers around the nation, the two greatest problems students face today are math classes and reading comprehension—and some of the math problems can even be attributed to poor reading skills.

How many times have you read to the bottom of a page or completed a section in a textbook and said to yourself, *"I don't remember a thing I just read."* In actuality, all of us have done this at one time or another. The strategies outlined in this lesson will help you eliminate this common occurrence from your study time. By applying these strategies, you will be able to read a page, a section, or an entire chapter so that when you reach the end, you will *comprehend and remember* what you just read.

DISCOVERING YOUR READING STYLE

Can Reading Become an Active Endeavor?

Active reading is really nothing more than a mindset. It is the attitude you have as you begin the reading process. For the next few days, try approaching your reading assignments with a positive, open-minded approach, and notice the difference in your own satisfaction, understanding, and overall comprehension. Instead of saying things like, "I hate reading" or "This stuff is worthless," reframe your self-talk into statements such as, "I'm going to learn from this" and "I think I can apply this to my life now." Using the assessment in Figure 7.1, take a moment and determine if your reading style is active or passive.

LEARNING TO BECOME AN ACTIVE READER

Can Reading Techniques, Speed, and Comprehension Be Improved?

As you begin to practice actively reading for comprehension, review the following tips to help you read material more quickly and understand it more clearly. Whenever you are faced with having to choose between *comprehension* or *speed*, choose comprehension! The following three tips will help as you begin to master reading college-level material:

Figure 7.1 Discovering Your Reading Style

Take a few moments and circle TRUE or FALSE for each of the statements below to determine if you are more of an active or passive reader.

1. I enjoy reading for pleasure.	TRUE	FALSE
2. College textbooks have little connection to my real life.	TRUE	FALSE
3. I look for the deeper meaning in words and phrases.	TRUE	FALSE
4. I seldom visualize what I am reading.	TRUE	FALSE
5. I look up words that I do not understand.	TRUE	FALSE
6. I read only what I have to read, and that is a stretch for me.	TRUE	FALSE
7. I stop reading to ponder what something means.	TRUE	FALSE
8. I never take notes when reading.	TRUE	FALSE
9. Reading brings me great joy.	TRUE	FALSE
10. My mind wanders constantly when I read.	TRUE	FALSE
11. I make time for reading even when I am not required to read.	TRUE	FALSE
12. Words are just words—they add no real meaning to my life or work.	TRUE	FALSE
13. I get excited about reading something new because I know I will learn something new and useful.	TRUE	FALSE
14. When reading, I just want to get it over with.	TRUE	FALSE
15. I usually have no trouble concentrating when reading.	TRUE	FALSE
16. I never look up words; I just read on.	TRUE	FALSE

Total of even-numbered TRUE responses _____

Total of odd-numbered TRUE responses _____

If you answered TRUE to more even numbers, you tend to be a more passive reader.

If you answered TRUE to more odd numbers, you tend to be a more active reader.

1. Learn to Concentrate

Speed and comprehension both require deep, ***mindful concentration***. Neither can be achieved without it. In order to comprehend information, your body needs to be ready to concentrate. You need sleep, rest, and proper nutrition. Most importantly, you need a quiet, peaceful place to concentrate on your reading. To increase your concentration and comprehension, consider the following:

- Reduce outside distractions, such as people talking, rooms that are too hot or cold, cell phones ringing, etc.

- Reduce internal distractions, such as fatigue, self-talk, daydreaming, hunger, and emotions that cause you to think of other things.
- Set a goal for reading a certain amount of material in an allotted time. This goal can help you focus.
- Take a short break every 20 minutes. Don't get distracted and do something else; come back to your reading in 3–5 minutes.
- Take notes as you read. This helps reading become an active process.
- When reading online material, don't become distracted by other technology, e-mails, Facebook posts, etc.

2. Overcome Fixation

Fixation is another important step in learning to read for speed and comprehension. Fixation is when your eyes stop on a single word to read it. Your eyes stop for only a fraction of a second, but those fractions add up over the course of a section or chapter. Your mind sees the words something like this:

Nutrition   is   important   to   good   health.

As you read this, you probably had six fixations because the words are spaced out. However, if they were not spaced, many people would still have six fixations. To increase your speed, try to see two or three words with one fixation; this will cut your reading time nearly in half. Try to see the sentence like this:

Nutrition is important   to good health.

Smith (2007) states: "Research has shown that the average reader can see approximately 2.5 words per fixation." To reduce your fixation time for active reading, consider the following:

- Practice seeing two or more words with one fixation.
- As you practice, try to read in phrases like the example below:

Nutrition is important   to good health.   Therefore,   you should work hard to eat proper meals every day.   By doing this you can maintain   good health

3. Combine Your Class and Text Notes

As you read material *before* you go to class, take notes on what you are reading. Look up unfamiliar words and paraphrase each paragraph in your notes. This helps you become actively involved and uses your critical thinking skills. While you are in class, take notes based on your instructor's lecture. Later that day (the earlier the better), take some time and compare/combine the notes from your readings with your classroom notes.

A helpful way to do this is to draw a line down the middle of the page. Place the notes from your text in the left column, and when you get to class, place your corresponding notes from the lecture in the right column. For example, if you read the section on effective ways to treat a blood clot in the text and your instructor begins to talk about this topic, place the instructor's lecture notes from class beside this topic from your text notes. This technique will allow you to compare the two sets of notes to determine if you have duplicate information or if you have omitted something important.

READING ONLINE MATERIAL
Are Different Reading Skills Required for Non-Print Materials?

Your may be asking, "Is reading online really different from reading the printed word?" The answer is yes, especially with today's online, interactive, multimedia environment. Not too long ago, college students purchased their books or reading packets from the college bookstore and read the printed word. Today, this is not typically the case. You may be required to download entire books or chapters, you may be assigned web sites to read and review by your instructors, and you will sometimes decide to explore topics further through online research. Reading online requires an adjusted set of skills. You will still need to use the reading tips in this chapter, especially SQ3R, but you will also need to familiarize yourself with the strategies for successfully reading online (non-textual) material. Consider the tips offered in Figure 7.2.

Figure 7.2 Tips for Reading Online Material

- Before you even open the site, plan some undisturbed time to survey, explore, and read the site. Make it a point to avoid distractions or multitasking, such as downloading songs on iTunes, reading your Facebook page, or checking e-mail. Devote this time to reading the material.

- Know why you are reading the online material.

- As you open the site, browse through (survey) it first to determine the length, view the main headings, and find out if you'll need to download plug-ins or any additional programs on your computer to access the material. Get a "feel" for the site and the material.

- Click on any menus or tabs to determine what additional information is available.

- Work to avoid eye strain. You can do this several ways:
  - Read in periods of 20 minutes. After 20 minutes, take a short break.
  - Increase the size of your view screen to make the site larger.
  - Copy the material, paste it into a Word document, and enlarge the font so that you can read it more clearly.

- While reading, use virtual sticky notes to mark important material. You can download several free sticky note programs by going online and searching "Free Online Sticky Notes."

- While reading, use an online highlighter to mark important material. To access an online highlighter, download one of the free online highlighting programs such as www.awesomehighlighter.com.

- While reading online, just as reading from printed material, take notes! This is one of the most important tools for memory and comprehension. As you read online material, take notes the traditional way or take virtual online notes. To do this, open a word-processing program, reduce it into the bottom menu bar, and as you read, click on it and add notes to your online page. Double space between each sentence to make it easier to read during your review period. You can also download several free online note-taking systems by searching "Free Online Note-Taking Software." You may want to consider investing in a dual monitor setup for your computer.

- Use free text-to-speech programs to convert your online material to verbal material. If you're on the run, download any free text-to-speech program and then copy and paste the written work into the program. Next, download the file to your mp3 player or burn it to a CD. You now have "reading on the run."

TAKING NOTES FROM READING MATERIAL

Can SQ3R Help Me Do It Right the First Time?

There are as many ways to approach a chapter in a textbook as there are students who read textbooks. Most would agree that there is no "right" or "wrong" way to begin the process. However, many would also agree that there are a few ways of approaching a chapter that are more effective than others. One such approach is SQ3R.

The most basic and often-used reading and studying system is the SQ3R method, developed by Francis P. Robinson in 1941. This simple, yet effective, system has proved to be a successful study tool for millions of students. SQ3R involves five steps: Scan, Question, Read, Recite, and Review. The most important thing to remember about SQ3R is that it should be used on a daily basis, not as a method for cramming. See Figure 7.3.

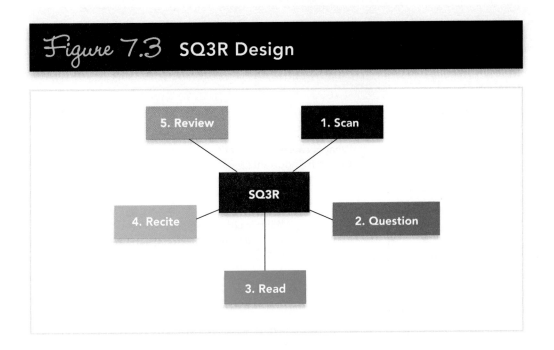

Figure 7.3 **SQ3R Design**

Step 1: Scan

The first step of SQ3R is to scan, or pre-read, an assigned chapter. You begin by reading the title of the chapter, the headings, and each sub-heading. Look carefully at the chapter objectives, vocabulary, time lines, graphs, charts, pictures, and drawings included in each chapter. If there is a chapter summary, read it. Scanning also includes reading the first and last sentence in each paragraph. Scanning is not a substitute for reading a chapter. Reading is discussed later. The steps for scanning a lesson or chapter might include answering the following questions:

What is the title of the chapter?

What is the subheading of the chapter?

List the chapter major headings.

What material is covered in boxed features?

If the chapter contains quotations, which one means the most to you? Why?

What is the most important graph or chart in the chapter? Why?

Close your book or website and list five topics that this chapter will cover.

Step 2: Question

The second step is to question. There are five common questions you should ask yourself when you are reading a chapter: Who? When? What? Where? and Why? As you scan and read your chapter, turn the information into questions and see if you can answer them. If you do not know the answers to the questions, you should find them as you read along.

Another way to approach the chapter is to turn the major headings of each section into questions (see an example in Figure 7.4). When you get to the end of the section, having

Figure 7.4 Forming Questions from Headings

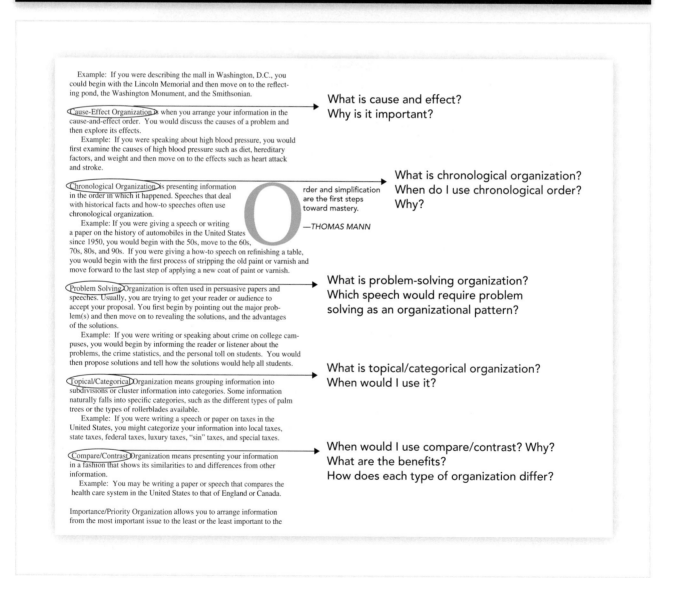

Example: If you were describing the mall in Washington, D.C., you could begin with the Lincoln Memorial and then move on to the reflecting pond, the Washington Monument, and the Smithsonian.

Cause-Effect Organization is when you arrange your information in the cause-and-effect order. You would discuss the causes of a problem and then explore its effects.

Example: If you were speaking about high blood pressure, you would first examine the causes of high blood pressure such as diet, hereditary factors, and weight and then move on to the effects such as heart attack and stroke.

→ **What is cause and effect?**
Why is it important?

Chronological Organization is presenting information in the order in which it happened. Speeches that deal with historical facts and how-to speeches often use chronological organization.

Example: If you were giving a speech or writing a paper on the history of automobiles in the United States since 1950, you would begin with the 50s, move to the 60s, 70s, 80s, and 90s. If you were giving a how-to speech on refinishing a table, you would begin with the first process of stripping the old paint or varnish and move forward to the last step of applying a new coat of paint or varnish.

→ **What is chronological organization?**
When do I use chronological order?
Why?

O*rder and simplification are the first steps toward mastery.*

—*THOMAS MANN*

Problem Solving Organization is often used in persuasive papers and speeches. Usually, you are trying to get your reader or audience to accept your proposal. You first begin by pointing out the major problem(s) and then move on to revealing the solutions, and the advantages of the solutions.

Example: If you were writing or speaking about crime on college campuses, you would begin by informing the reader or listener about the problems, the crime statistics, and the personal toll on students. You would then propose solutions and tell how the solutions would help all students.

→ **What is problem-solving organization?**
Which speech would require problem solving as an organizational pattern?

Topical/Categorical Organization means grouping information into subdivisions or cluster information into categories. Some information naturally falls into specific categories, such as the different types of palm trees or the types of rollerblades available.

Example: If you were writing a speech or paper on taxes in the United States, you might categorize your information into local taxes, state taxes, federal taxes, luxury taxes, "sin" taxes, and special taxes.

→ **What is topical/categorical organization?**
When would I use it?

Compare/Contrast Organization means presenting your information in a fashion that shows its similarities to and differences from other information.

Example: You may be writing a paper or speech that compares the health care system in the United States to that of England or Canada.

→ **When would I use compare/contrast? Why?**
What are the benefits?
How does each type of organization differ?

Importance/Priority Organization allows you to arrange information from the most important issue to the least or the least important to the

carefully read the material, taken notes, and highlighted important information, answer the question that you posed at the beginning of the section.

Step 3: Read

After you scan the chapter and develop some questions to be answered from the chapter, the next step is to read the chapter. Remember, scanning is not reading. There is no substitute for reading in your success plan. Read slowly and carefully. The SQ3R method requires a substantial amount of time, but if you take each step slowly and completely, you will be amazed at how much you can learn and how much your grades will improve.

"There are worse crimes than burning books. One of them is not reading them."
—Joseph Brodsky

Read through each section. It is best not to jump around or move ahead if you do not understand the previous section. Paragraphs are usually built on each other, and so you need to understand the first before you can move on to the next. You may have to read a chapter or section more than once, especially if the information is new, technical, or difficult.

Take notes, highlight, and make marginal notes in your textbook as you read along. You own your textbook and should personalize it as you would your lecture notes. Highlight areas that you feel are important, underline words and phrases that you did not understand or that you feel are important, and jot down notes in the margins.

As you begin to read your chapter, mark the text, and take notes, keep the following in mind:

- Read the entire paragraph before you mark anything.
- Identify the topic or thesis statement of each paragraph and highlight it.
- Highlight key phrases.
- Don't highlight too much; the text will lose its significance. See Figure 7.5.
- Use two different color highlighters—one for "important information" and one for "very interesting information."
- Stop and look up words that you do not know or understand.

While reading, you will want to take notes that are more elaborate than your highlighting or marginal notes. Taking notes while reading the text will assist you in studying the material and committing it to memory. **This is a major part of *learning actively*.** There are several effective methods of taking notes while reading (see Figure 7.6). They include:

Charts	Outlines
Flashcards	Mind maps
Time lines	Summaries
Key words	

As you read through a chapter in your textbook, you may find that you have to use a variety of these techniques to capture information. Try them for one week. Although taking notes while reading a chapter thoroughly is time consuming, you will be amazed at how much you remember and how much you are able to contribute in class after using these techniques. It works!

Step 4: Recite

Recitation is simple but crucial. Skipping this step may result in less than full mastery of the chapter. Once you have read a section using one or more of the techniques from above, ask yourself this simple question: *"What was that all about?"* Find a classmate, sit down together,

Figure 7.5 **The Downlow on Highlighting**

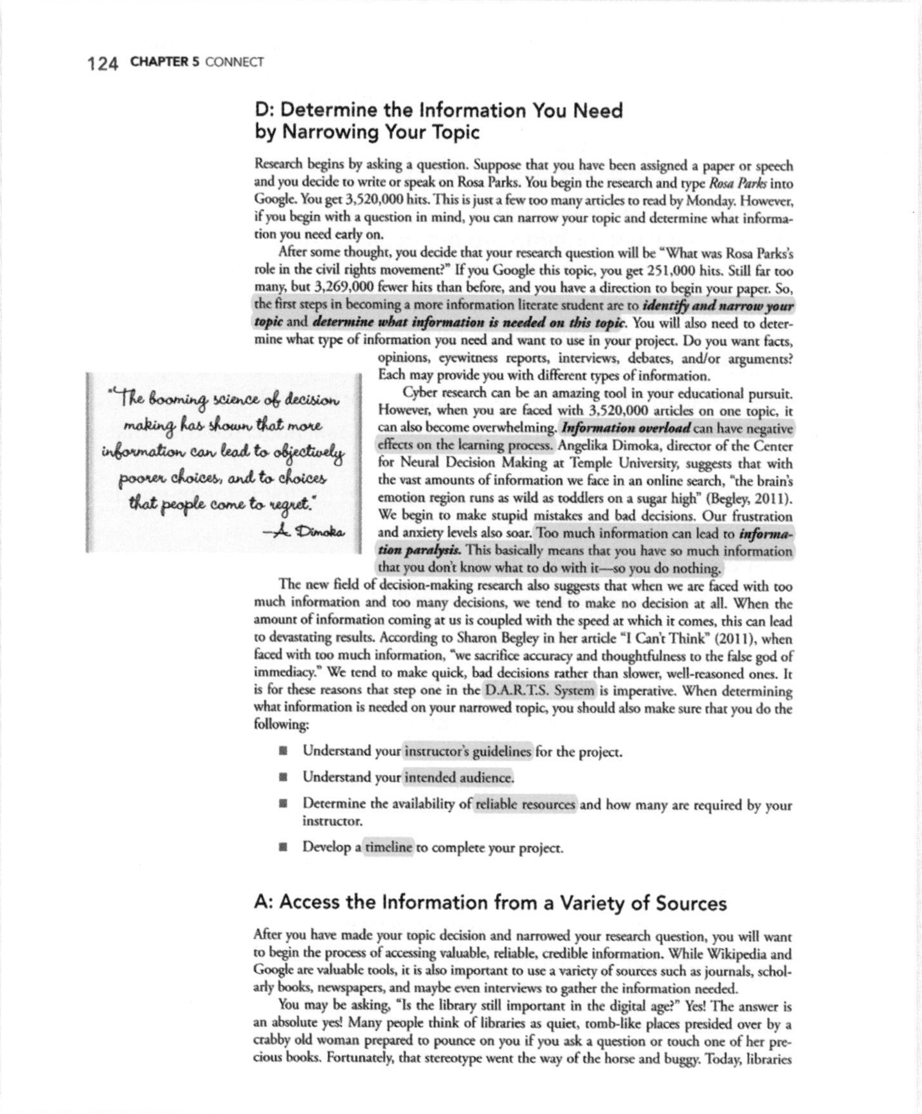

D: Determine the Information You Need by Narrowing Your Topic

Research begins by asking a question. Suppose that you have been assigned a paper or speech and you decide to write or speak on Rosa Parks. You begin the research and type *Rosa Parks* into Google. You get 3,520,000 hits. This is just a few too many articles to read by Monday. However, if you begin with a question in mind, you can narrow your topic and determine what information you need early on.

After some thought, you decide that your research question will be "What was Rosa Parks's role in the civil rights movement?" If you Google this topic, you get 251,000 hits. Still far too many, but 3,269,000 fewer hits than before, and you have a direction to begin your paper. So, the first steps in becoming a more information literate student are to *identify and narrow your topic* and *determine what information is needed on this topic.* You will also need to determine what type of information you need and want to use in your project. Do you want facts, opinions, eyewitness reports, interviews, debates, and/or arguments? Each may provide you with different types of information.

Cyber research can be an amazing tool in your educational pursuit. However, when you are faced with 3,520,000 articles on one topic, it can also become overwhelming. *Information overload* can have negative effects on the learning process. Angelika Dimoka, director of the Center for Neural Decision Making at Temple University, suggests that with the vast amounts of information we face in an online search, "the brain's emotion region runs as wild as toddlers on a sugar high" (Begley, 2011). We begin to make stupid mistakes and bad decisions. Our frustration and anxiety levels also soar. Too much information can lead to *information paralysis.* This basically means that you have so much information that you don't know what to do with it—so you do nothing.

> "The booming science of decision making has shown that more information can lead to objectively poorer choices, and to choices that people come to regret."
>
> —A. Dimoka

The new field of decision-making research also suggests that when we are faced with too much information and too many decisions, we tend to make no decision at all. When the amount of information coming at us is coupled with the speed at which it comes, this can lead to devastating results. According to Sharon Begley in her article "I Can't Think" (2011), when faced with too much information, "we sacrifice accuracy and thoughtfulness to the false god of immediacy." We tend to make quick, bad decisions rather than slower, well-reasoned ones. It is for these reasons that step one in the D.A.R.T.S. System is imperative. When determining what information is needed on your narrowed topic, you should also make sure that you do the following:

- Understand your instructor's guidelines for the project.
- Understand your intended audience.
- Determine the availability of reliable resources and how many are required by your instructor.
- Develop a timeline to complete your project.

A: Access the Information from a Variety of Sources

After you have made your topic decision and narrowed your research question, you will want to begin the process of accessing valuable, reliable, credible information. While Wikipedia and Google are valuable tools, it is also important to use a variety of sources such as journals, scholarly books, newspapers, and maybe even interviews to gather the information needed.

You may be asking, "Is the library still important in the digital age?" Yes! The answer is an absolute yes! Many people think of libraries as quiet, tomb-like places presided over by a crabby old woman prepared to pounce on you if you ask a question or touch one of her precious books. Fortunately, that stereotype went the way of the horse and buggy. Today, libraries

and ask questions of each other. Discuss with each other the main points of the chapter. Try to explain the information to each other without looking at your notes. If you are at home, sit back in your chair, recite the information, and determine what it means. If you have trouble explaining the information to your friend or reciting it to yourself, you probably did not understand the section and you should go back and re-read it. If you can tell your classmate and yourself exactly what you just read and what it means, you are ready to move on to the next section of the chapter.

Figure 7.6   Sample Note-Taking Methods

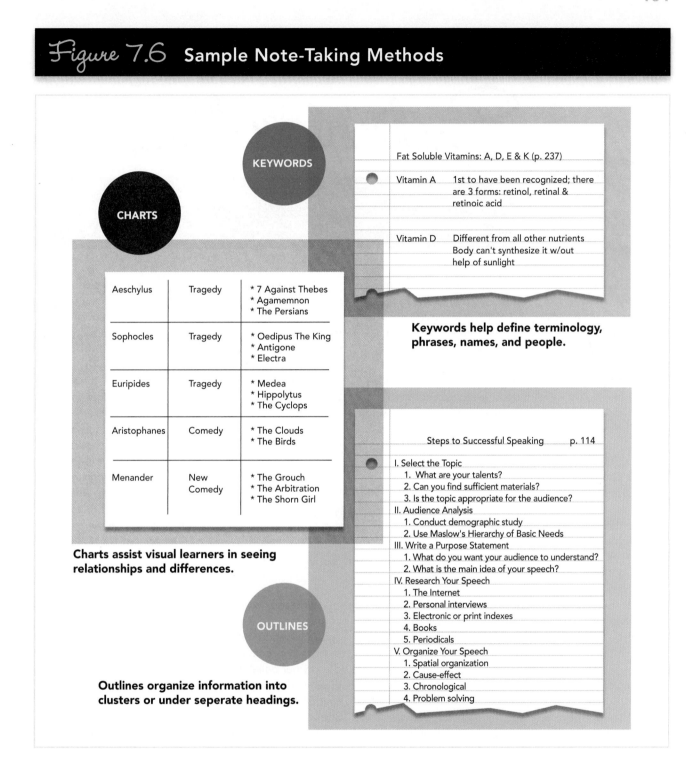

KEYWORDS

Fat Soluble Vitamins: A, D, E & K (p. 237)

Vitamin A   1st to have been recognized; there are 3 forms: retinol, retinal & retinoic acid

Vitamin D   Different from all other nutrients Body can't synthesize it w/out help of sunlight

Keywords help define terminology, phrases, names, and people.

CHARTS

Aeschylus	Tragedy	* 7 Against Thebes * Agamemnon * The Persians
Sophocles	Tragedy	* Oedipus The King * Antigone * Electra
Euripides	Tragedy	* Medea * Hippolytus * The Cyclops
Aristophanes	Comedy	* The Clouds * The Birds
Menander	New Comedy	* The Grouch * The Arbitration * The Shorn Girl

Charts assist visual learners in seeing relationships and differences.

OUTLINES

Steps to Successful Speaking   p. 114

I. Select the Topic
   1. What are your talents?
   2. Can you find sufficient materials?
   3. Is the topic appropriate for the audience?
II. Audience Analysis
   1. Conduct demographic study
   2. Use Maslow's Hierarchy of Basic Needs
III. Write a Purpose Statement
   1. What do you want your audience to understand?
   2. What is the main idea of your speech?
IV. Research Your Speech
   1. The Internet
   2. Personal interviews
   3. Electronic or print indexes
   4. Books
   5. Periodicals
V. Organize Your Speech
   1. Spatial organization
   2. Cause-effect
   3. Chronological
   4. Problem solving

Outlines organize information into clusters or under seperate headings.

Step 5: Review

After you have read the chapter, immediately go back and read it again. **"What?! I just read it!"** Yes, you did. And the best way to determine whether you have mastered the information is to once again survey the chapter; review marginal notes, highlighted areas, and vocabulary words; and determine whether you can answer the questions you posed during the "Question Step" of SQ3R. This step will help you store and retain this information in long-term memory.

from **ordinary** to

Extraordinary

Lydia Hausler Lebovic, Jewish Holocaust Survivor, Auschwitz
Concentration/Extermination Camp, Auschwitz, Poland, 1944

She was "sweet sixteen." The time of joy for so many female teens today. It is a milestone date when childhood passes and young adulthood arrives. One can legally drive, and in many states, "sweet sixteen" signifies the age of consent.

Lydia Hausler Lebovic's "sweet sixteen" was very different, however. Like many young ladies, she was dating, had a somewhat rebellious relationship with her mother, and socialized with friends, but in the countryside around her, World War II raged. In 1944 when she was 16, she and her family were ordered to pack 20 pounds of personal belongings and told they were being taken to "the Ghetto," a holding area for Jews in her hometown of Uzhorod, Czechoslovakia, now a part of Ukraine. She understood that the situation was not good and that things were changing, but Lydia had no real idea of how her life would forever be altered in the coming weeks, months, and years.

After two weeks in "the Ghetto," Lydia, her family, friends, and neighbors were ordered onto cattle cars—60 to 80 per car—and told that they were being taken to Hungary to work in the corn and wheat fields. So there, in the darkness of night, her horrific journey began—young, old, weak, strong, nursing mothers, and babies—all in the same cattle car with no water and only two buckets to use for a bathroom. After two days of travel, the train stopped and the doors of the cattle car opened. Her greatest fear had come to reality. They were at Auschwitz Concentration Camp.

When the doors of the cattle cars opened, the men were quickly separated from the women, and the children from the adults. They were put into lines of five and marched forward. In front of every line was an SS officer. Quickly, Lydia was pushed to the right and her mother and sister were pushed to the left. Little did she know at that point that those shoved to the right would be put to work and those shoved to the left would be dead by the evening. She never saw her mother or sister again after that moment. She never said goodbye. She was "sweet sixteen."

> *Little did she know at that point that those shoved to the right would be put to work and those shoved to the left would be dead by the evening.*

After being taken to barracks where 12–14 people slept in a bed, Lydia approached one of the older females being held. She asked her, "When do I get to see my mother and my sister?" The older lady took Lydia by the arm and pointed toward the billowing chimney of the crematory. *"You see that smoke? You see that ash? You smell that flesh burning? That's your mother. That's your sister."* Lydia tried not to believe her, but it was absolutely true. Her mother and sister were gassed and cremated.

She remained in Auschwitz until she was shipped to the labor camp, Bergen-Belsen, in Germany. She was liberated on April 15, 1945. Upon liberation, she began working for the British Red Cross where she was reunited with a friend of her brother. They were married in November of 1945. They moved to Chile in 1947, and then to Los Angeles, CA, in 1963.

Lydia now travels the nation speaking about the events of her life and delivering the message "Never Again." Lydia's life and determination are proof that the Holocaust did not ruin her. They did not destroy her. They did not destroy her belief in love. They did not destroy her faith in people. They did not destroy her religion or values. The events made her a stronger, more compassionate person. She went on to become a loving wife and mother, a successful businesswoman, and eventually a devoted grandmother. *She refused to be ruined.* She moved from ordinary to extraordinary.

EXTRAORDINARY REFLECTION

Mrs. Lebovic suffered the death of family members during the Holocaust but she makes the point in her presentations, "The Holocaust did not ruin me. They did not destroy me. They did not destroy my belief in love. I refused to be ruined." How can adversity in your life, like that in Mrs. Lebovic's, make you a stronger and more motivated person?

REFLECTIONS
on Reading and Comprehension

SQ3R can be a lifesaver when it comes to understanding material that is overwhelming. It is an efficient, comprehensive, and *doable* practice that can dramatically assist you in your reading efforts. It may take more time than your old method, but you will begin to see the results almost immediately. Seriously considering and practicing the strategies outlined in this chapter will help increase your comprehension level and it will also help your ability to recall the information when you need it later on.

READING FOR COMPREHENSION

Each lesson-end assessment is based on Bloom's Taxonomy of Learning. See the first page of this lesson for a quick review.

This activity uses levels 1–6 of the taxonomy

Read the following article. While reading, practice the SQ3R technique. First, *scan* the article, then, using your notebook or online note-taking system, write at least two *questions* that you think will be important to mastering this material. Now, *read* the article article, highlighting words and phrases, looking up words you do not understand, and paraphrasing each paragraph. Then, without looking at your notes or the article, *recite* what you have just read. *Review* the article to ensure that you did not miss anything in your notes or recitation. Finally, in 100 words or less, thoroughly *summarize* this entire article. Be certain to include facts, statistics, main points, and tips. Pretend that you have to explain this entire article to someone who knows nothing about the effects of poor sleep.

WHAT'S SLEEP
GOT TO DO WITH IT?

You've heard the old saying, "You are what you eat." This may be true, but many sleep experts would say, "You are how you sleep." Sleep deprivation is one of the leading causes of poor productivity and academic performance, workplace and auto accidents, lack of concentration, diminished immune systems, decreased metabolism, cardiovascular problems, and even poor communication efforts.

The National Traffic Safety Administration estimates that 100,000 crashes each year are the result of sleepy drivers. These crashes cause nearly 1600 deaths, 71,000 injuries, and $12.5 billion in property loss and diminished activity ("Hidden Menace," 2003).

Mark Rosekind, Ph.D., an expert on fatigue and performance issues and a member of the board of directors for the National Sleep Foundation, states, "Without sufficient sleep it is more difficult to concentrate, make careful decisions, and follow instructions; we are more likely to make mistakes or errors, and are more prone to being impatient and lethargic. Our attention, memory, and reaction time are all affected" (Cardinal, 2003).

According to the National Sleep Foundation, the following symptoms can signal inadequate sleep:

- Dozing off while engaged in an activity such as reading, watching TV, sitting in meetings, or sitting in traffic.
- Slowed thinking and reacting.
- Difficulty listening to what is said or understanding directions.
- Difficulty remembering or retaining information.
- Frequent errors or mistakes.
- Narrowing of attention, missing important changes in a situation.
- Depression or negative mood.
- Impatience or being quick to anger.
- Frequent blinking, difficulty focusing eyes, or heavy eyelids.

Indeed, lack of sleep can decrease your ability to study, recall information, and perform well on tests and assignments. This can be especially true during midterm and final exam periods. Those late or all-night cram sessions can actually be more detrimental to your academic success than helpful. By including your study sessions in your time-management plan, you can avoid having to spend your sleep time studying.

Different people need different amounts of sleep within a 24-hour period. Some people absolutely need 8–10 hours of sleep, while others can function well on 4–6 hours. If you are not sleeping enough to rest and revive your body, you will experience sleep deprivation.

Researchers suggest that missing as little as 2 hours of sleep for *one* night can take as long as 6 days to recover—if it is recovered at all (Mass, 1990). It is generally estimated that 8–9 hours of *good, solid, restful* sleep per night can decrease your chances of sleep deprivation.

Below, you will find some helpful hints for getting a good night's rest:

- Avoid alcohol and caffeine (yes, alcohol is a depressant, but it interrupts both REM and slow-wave sleep, and caffeine can stay in your system for as long as 12 hours).
- Exercise during the day (but not within four hours of your sleep time).
- Regulate the temperature in your bedroom to a comfortable setting for you.
- Wind down before trying to sleep. Complete all tasks at least one hour prior to your bedtime. This gives you time to relax and prepare for rest.
- Avoid taking naps during the day.
- Have a set bedtime and try to stick to it.
- Take a warm bath before bedtime.
- Go to bed only when you are tired. If you are not asleep within 15–30 minutes, get up and do something restful like reading or listening to soft music.
- Use relaxation techniques such as visualization and mind travel.
- Avoid taking sleeping aids. This can cause more long-term problems than sleep deprivation.

REFERENCE

Smith, B. (2007). *Breaking Through: College Reading* (7th ed.). Upper Saddle River, NJ: Pearson Education.

lesson eight
STUDY

DEVELOPING YOUR MEMORY, STUDYING, AND TEST-TAKING SKILLS

Fotolia

"We can learn something new at any time we believe we can." —Virginia Satir

Why read this lesson?

Because you'll learn how to:

- Recommend strategies for studying for and taking a test

Because you'll be able to:

- Describe effective study habits
- Identify various memory strategies for studying
- Analyze strategies for taking different types of tests

Knowledge in Bloom

Bloom's Taxonomy of Learning is a simple way of explaining the levels at which we all learn material and acquire information. The learning levels progress from basic to more complex learning and thinking. Examples are detailed below. Throughout this lesson, you'll see colorful triangles to the side of some activities. They let you know on which level of Bloom's Taxonomy the questions are based.

- **LEVEL 1: Remember**
  List three effective study habits.
- **LEVEL 2: Understand**
  Discuss memory strategies that improve learning.
- **LEVEL 3: Apply**
  Demonstrate your understanding of mnemonics.
- **LEVEL 4: Analyze**
  Compare and contrast VCR3 and SQ3R.
- **LEVEL 5: Evaluate**
  Recommend strategies for forming a study group.
- **LEVEL 6: Create**
  Design a plan for taking essay tests.

MyStudentSuccessLab

MyStudentSuccessLab is an online solution designed to help you acquire and develop (or hone) the skills you need to succeed. You will have access to peer-led video presentations and develop core skills through interactive exercises and projects.

DEVELOPING EFFECTIVE STUDY HABITS

Can All This Studying Be Effectively Managed?

Let's face it—studying is not much fun for most people. Effective studying is a skill that requires listening, reading, time management, self-discipline, organization, recall, recitation, and outlining. So how do you develop effective study habits when you just plain don't like to study?

- **First, you have to study smarter, and you have to have a system.** You can't make yourself want to study, so you have to get in the right frame of mind. This means thinking positively about studying, telling yourself that you will do well, and that you are learning valuable skills and knowledge. You have to avoid saying negative things to yourself, for example, "I know I am going to fail this test."

- **Find a good place to study that has no distractions.** Turn off the TV and loud music, and get away from boisterous friends who disturb your concentration. If you can study at home, this is fine, but you have to find a quiet place that is conducive to studying and learning. You might try a cubicle in the library or a quiet coffee shop. Go to this place every time you study so you get comfortable with your surroundings. Don't answer the phone during your study time!

- **Keep all the things you need to study effectively in the same place if you study at home so you don't have to jump up and down and waste time.** Do you need your computer? Do you have paper and pencils? What about your textbook? Did you bring your notes? Do you need your iPad or iPod or calculator? Do you need a dictionary or thesaurus?

- **Read the material before you go to class.** You are much more likely to understand what the instructor is discussing if you have read the chapter before class.

- **Take good notes in class and try to go over them as soon as possible after you leave class.** Immediately after class is the best time to study. Make corrections. If something is missing, try to get it from a classmate. Outline your notes. Some people even like to re-write them. Others like to put notes in groups that seem to go together; this is called chunking. Think about how you learn best. Is it from reading notes or do you learn best by talking out loud?

- **Preview the chapter.** Pay attention to major headings, sub-headings, italicized words, pictures, diagrams, and end-of-chapter exercises. Make notes in your textbook.

- **Use the SQ3R method of studying.** This means: survey, question, read, recite, and review.

- **Visualize what you are studying and trying to learn.** Using colored pens helps some people remember specific items. Draw pictures, diagrams, and maps—use anything that helps you learn and recall information.

- **Form a study group of people in your class** who seem to be interested in making good grades. Keep the group small. Take practice tests that your group composes from all your notes.

> "Studies show that as much as 80% of material learned in class is forgotten within 24 hours if there is no review."
> —Maryland Community College SOAR Program

- **If old exams from the same professor are available, by all means, study them.** Some of the questions will be similar, but don't count on the old exam being just like the one you will be taking.

- **Design a schedule for studying each of your courses and stick to it.** If you do this every day, you will learn and remember more. Cramming rarely works, but systematic studying and reciting and outlining do work. Schedule long-term projects and allow yourself enough time to do them well.

- **Study at your peak performance time if possible.** Some people learn best early in the morning, while others learn best in the evening. No one learns best by pulling all-nighters.

- **Study your most difficult subjects first, and the ones you like the least.** With these out of the way, you will feel like a weight has been lifted from your head.

- **Reward yourself when you have studied carefully and thoroughly.** Take a break and go for a walk or watch a short TV program. Say something to yourself like: "When I study for an hour, I will play my new video game for 30 minutes."

USING MEMORY STRATEGIES TO IMPROVE LEARNING

Do Memory Tricks Really Work?

This section will detail how memory works and why it is important to your studying efforts. Psychologists have determined that there are three types of memory: **sensory** memory; **short-term, or working** memory; and **long-term** memory.

Sensory memory stores information gathered from the five senses: taste, touch, smell, hearing, and sight. Sensory memory is usually temporary, lasting about one to three seconds, unless you decide that the information is of ultimate importance to you and make an effort to transfer it to long-term memory. **Short-term, or working memory** holds information for a short amount of time. Consider the following list of letters:

jmplngtoplntstsevng

Now, cover them with your hand and try to recite them.

It is almost impossible for the average person to do so. Why? Because your working memory bank can hold a limited amount of information, usually about five to nine separate new facts or pieces of information at once (Woolfolk, 2006). However, consider this exercise. If you break the letters down into smaller pieces and add *meaning* to them, you are more likely to retain them. Example:

jum   lng   to   plnts   ts   evng

This may still not mean very much to you, but you can probably remember at least the first two sets of information—jum lng.

Now, if you were to say to yourself, this sentence means: Jump Long To Planets This Evening, you are much more likely to begin to remember this information. Just as your memory can "play tricks" on you, you can "play tricks" on your memory.

Long-term memory stores a lot of information. It is almost like a hard drive on your computer. You have to make an effort to put something in your long-term memory, but with effort and memory techniques, such as rehearsal, practice, and mnemonic devices, you can store anything you want to remember there.

MORE MEMORY STRATEGIES

What Does a Greek Goddess Have to Do with My Memory?

One of the most effective memory strategies is using mnemonics. The word *mnemonics* is derived from the Greek goddess of memory, Mnemosyne (pronounced ne-mo-ze-knee). She was considered one of the most important goddesses of all time because it was believed that memory separated us from lower animal life forms. It was believed that memory was the very foundation of civilization (Monaghan, 2009). Memory was so very important because most of the transmission of human history depended on oral stories and parables committed only to memory, not on paper. Take a moment and review the first photo in Figure 8.1. Then view the photo with notations, and answer the questions that follow. How well did you remember the details of what you had observed?

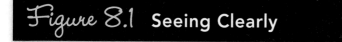

Figure 8.1   Seeing Clearly

Consider this picture. Study it carefully.
Look at everything from left to right, top to bottom.

Sonya Etchison/Fotolia

Now, notice the picture and pay close attention to the areas marked.

Notice the people on the trampoline   Notice the storage building

Notice the color of the protective padding

Notice the green foliage

Notice the utility meter

Level 1 Remember

Now, cover this picture and answer the following questions:

1. How many people are on the trampoline? _____

2. What color is the protective padding on the edge? _____

3. What is the season of the year based on the foliage color? _____

4. What colors are used on the storage building? _____

5. Is there one utility meter or two? _____

6. How many children are in the air? _____

7. Are the children all male, female, or mixed? _____

8. How many people are wearing striped shirts? _____

9. What type of fence surrounds the house? _____

10. What colors are used on the house? _____

11. Is the house made of one material or more? _____

12. What color are the flowers on the bush? _____

"NOT FAIR!," you might say. "You did not tell us to look at the house or the color of the flowers." The purpose of this activity is to show you the difference between just looking at something and really reviewing it. To truly learn something and commit it to memory, you have to go beyond surface learning and reading.

In modern times, a ***mnemonic device*** (pronounced **ni**-mŏn-ik) is a memory trick or technique that assists you in putting information into your long-term memory and pulling it out when you need it. According to research into mnemonics and their effectiveness, it was found that mnemonics can help create a phenomenon known as the ***bizarreness effect***. This effect causes us to remember information that is "bizarre" or unusual more rapidly than "normal," everyday facts. "The bizarreness effect occurs because unusual information and events trigger heightened levels of our attention and require us to work harder to make sense of them; thus we remember the information and its associated interaction better" (McCornack, 2007).

The following types of mnemonic devices may help you with your long-term memory:

JINGLES/RHYMES. You can make up rhymes, songs, poems, or sayings to assist you in remembering information. For example, "Columbus sailed the ocean blue in fourteen hundred and ninety-two."

SENTENCES. You can make up sentences to help you remember information. For example, "**M**y **V**ery **E**lderly **M**other **J**ust **S**aved **U**s **N**icely" is a mnemonic for the eight planets in order from the sun (Mercury, Venus, Earth, Mars, Jupiter, Saturn, Uranus, Neptune). Another example is "**P**lease **e**xcuse **m**y **d**ear **A**unt **S**ally," which corresponds to the order of mathematical operations: **p**arentheses, **e**xponents, **m**ultiplication, **d**ivision, **a**ddition, and **s**ubtraction.

ACRONYMS. An acronym is a word that is formed from the first letters of other words. You may see re-runs for the famed TV show *M*A*S*H*. This is an acronym for Mobile Army Surgical Hospital. If you scuba dive, you know that *SCUBA* is an acronym for Self-Contained Underwater Breathing Apparatus.

THE VCR3 MEMORY TECHNIQUE
How Can VCR3 Increase Memory Power?

Countless pieces of information are stored in your long-term memory. Some of it is triggered by necessity, some may be triggered by the five senses, and some may be triggered by experiences. The best way to commit information to long-term memory and retrieve it when needed can be expressed by:

V Visualizing
C Concentrating
R Relating
R Repeating
R Reviewing

Consider the following story:

As Katherine walked to her car after her evening class, she heard someone behind her. She turned to see two students holding hands walking about 20 feet behind her. She was relieved. This was the first night that she had walked to her car alone.

Katherine pulled her book bag closer to her as she increased her pace along the dimly lit sidewalk between the Salk Biology Building and the Horn Center for the Arts. "I can't believe that Shana didn't call me," she thought to herself. "She knows I hate to walk to the parking lot alone."

As Katherine turned the corner onto Suddith Street, she heard someone else behind her. She turned but did not see anyone. As she continued to walk toward her car, she heard the sound again. Turning to see if anyone was there, she saw a shadow disappear into the grove of hedges along the sidewalk.

Startled and frightened, Katherine crossed the street to walk beneath the streetlights and sped up to get closer to a group of students about 30 feet in front of her. She turned once more to see if anyone was behind her. Thankfully, she did not see anyone.

By this time, she was very close to her car. The lighting was better and other students were around. She felt better, but vowed never again to leave class alone at night.

STEP 1: VISUALIZE. As you read Katherine's story, were you able to visualize her journey? Could you see her walking along the sidewalk? Did you see the two buildings? What did they look like? Could you see the darkness of her path? Could you see that shadow disappearing into the bushes? Could you see her increasing her pace to catch up to the other students? What was she wearing?

If you did this, then you are using your visual skills—your *mind's eye*. This is one of the most effective ways to commit information to long-term memory. See it, live it, feel it, and touch it as you read and study it, and it will become yours.

STEP 2: CONCENTRATE. Concentrating on the information given will help you commit it to long-term memory. Don't let your mind wander. Stay focused. If you find yourself having trouble concentrating, take a small break (two to five minutes) and then go back to work.

STEP 3: RELATE. Relating the information to something that you already know or understand will assist you in filing or storing the information for easy retrieval. Relating the appearance of the African zebra to the American horse can help you remember what the zebra looks like. You may not know what the building in Katherine's story looked like, but try to see her in front of a building at your school. Creating these types of relationships increases memory retention of the material.

STEP 4: REPEAT. Repeating the information out loud to yourself or to a study partner facilitates its transfer to long-term memory. Some people have to hear information many times before they can commit it to long-term memory. Memory experts agree that repetition is one of the **strongest** tools to increase the retention of material.

STEP 5: REVIEW. Reviewing the information is another means of repetition. The more you see and use the information, the easier it will be to remember it when the time comes. As you review, try to remember the main points of the information.

Level 1 Remember

Without looking back, answer the following questions about Katherine. Use the power of your visualization and concentration to recall the information.

1. What was the name of the biology building?

   _____

2. Did she see the shadow before or after she saw the two people behind her?

   _____

3. What were the two people behind her doing?

   _____

4. What was the name of the arts building?

   _____

USING STUDY GROUPS

Can Study Groups Assist in Learning?

There may be situations where you will need or want to study in a group. You may find a study group at your institution or your may establish a study group online through your Learning Management System discussion board, Skype, WebEx, or other electronic meeting sites.

The following tips will help you when you establish or join a study group:

- Limit the number of participants to 3–5 people and spend some time getting acquainted. Exchange contact information if you're comfortable doing so.
- Each member should make a personal commitment to bring their best to the group each time you meet, and they must make an effort to make a contribution.
- Limit the group to those people who can meet at the specified times, dates, and locations.
- Set rules so that all members know the objectives and goals of the study period.
- Limit the study time to 2–3 hours—longer periods tend to be less productive.
- All members of the group should prepare, share, and participate.
- The study group should have a goal for each session.
- Assignments should be made for the next study session so that everyone comes prepared and you can cover the material that needs to be learned.
- Select a leader so that you reach your goals during the meeting.

THINKING ABOUT TESTING

Can an Attitude Adjustment Help Reduce Text Anxiety?

Yes, an attitude adjustment may be necessary to help you get you through tests. A positive or negative attitude can truly mean the difference between success and failure. With an attitude adjustment from negative to positive and some basic preparation, you can overcome a good deal of your anxiety about tests and do well. You can reduce anxiety when you are in control of the situation, and you can gain control by convincing yourself that you *can be* and *will be* successful.

What Questions Should I Ask Before the Test?

Several classes before the test is scheduled **quiz your instructor** about the logistics and specifics of the test. This information can help you study more effectively and eliminate the anxiety that comes with uncertainty. If you don't know if the test is going to be true-false or essay or both, it is much more difficult to study. Some questions you need to ask are:

Do you find that studying in the library, at home, or somewhere else is most effective for you? Why?

Diego Cervo/Shutterstock

1. What type of questions will be on the test?
2. How many questions will be on the test?
3. Is there a time limit on the test?
4. Will there be any special instructions, such as use pen only or use a number 2 pencil?
5. Is there a study sheet?
6. Will there be a review session?
7. What is the grade value of the test?
8. What chapters or sections will the test cover?

TEST-TAKING STRATEGIES AND HINTS FOR SUCCESS

What Happens When the Answers Just Won't Come?

Almost every test question will elicit one of three types of responses from you as the test taker:

Quick-time response   Lag-time response   No Response

Your response is a *quick-time response* when you read a question and know the answer immediately. You may need to read only one key word in the test question to know the correct response. Even if you have a quick-time response, however, always read the entire question before answering.

You have a *lag-time response* when you read a question and the answer does not come to you immediately. You may have to read the question several times or even move on to another question before you think of the correct response. Information in another question will sometimes trigger the response you need. Don't get nervous if you have a lag-time response.

No response is the least desirable situation when you are taking a test. You may read a question two or three times and still have no response. At this point, you should move on to another question to try to find some related information. When this happens, you have some options:

1. Leave this question until the very end of the test.
2. Make an intelligent guess.
3. Try to eliminate all unreasonable answers by association.
4. Watch for modifiers within the question.

Tips for Test Taking

Before you read about the strategies for answering these different types of questions, think about this: *There is no substitute for studying!* You can know all the tips, ways to reduce anxiety, mnemonics, and strategies on Earth, but if you have not studied, they will be of little help to you.

Strategies for Matching Questions

Matching questions frequently involve knowledge of people, dates, places, or vocabulary. When answering matching questions, you should:

- Read the directions and each column carefully before you answer.
- Determine whether the two columns have an equal number of items.
- Match what you know first, and cross off information that is already used.
- Use the process of elimination for answers you might not know.
- Look for logical clues.
- Use the longer statement as a question; use the shorter statement as an answer.

Strategies for True–False Questions

True–false questions ask if a statement is true or not. True–false questions can be some of the trickiest questions ever developed. Some students like them; some hate them. There is a 50/50 chance of answering correctly, but you can use the following strategies to increase your odds on true–false tests:

- Read each statement carefully.
- Watch for key words in each statement, for example, negatives.
- Read each statement for double negatives, such as "not untruthful."
- Pay attention to words that may indicate that a statement is true, such as "some," "few," "many," and "often."
- Pay attention to words that may indicate that a statement is false, such as "never," "all," "every," and "only."
- Remember that if any part of a statement is false, the entire statement is false.
- Answer every question unless there is a penalty for guessing.

Strategies for Multiple-Choice Questions

Many college instructors give multiple-choice tests because they are easy to grade and provide quick, precise responses. A multiple-choice question asks you to choose from among usually two to five answers to complete a sentence. Some strategies for increasing your success in answering multiple-choice questions are the following:

- Read the question and try to answer it before you read the answers provided.
- Look for similar answers; one of them is usually the correct response.
- Recognize that answers containing extreme modifiers, such as *always, every,* and *never,* are usually wrong.
- Cross off answers that you know are incorrect.
- Read all the options before selecting your answer. Even if you believe that A is the correct response, read them all.
- Recognize that when the answers are all numbers, the highest and lowest numbers are usually incorrect.
- Recognize that a joke is usually wrong.
- Understand that the most inclusive answer is often correct.
- Understand that the longest answer is often correct.
- If you cannot answer a question, move on to the next one and continue through the test; another question may trigger the answer you missed.
- Answer every question unless there is a penalty for guessing.

Strategies for Short-Answer Questions

Short-answer questions, also called fill-in-the-blanks, ask you to supply the answer yourself, not to select it from a list. Although "short answer" sounds easy, these questions are often very difficult. Short-answer questions require you to draw from your long-term memory. The following hints can help you answer this type of question successfully:

- Read each question and be sure that you know what is being asked.
- Be brief in your response.
- Give the same number of answers as there are blanks; for example, _____ and _____ would require two answers.
- Never assume that the length of the blank has anything to do with the length of the answer.
- Remember that your initial response is usually correct.
- Pay close attention to the word immediately preceding the blank; if the word is "an," give a response that begins with a vowel (*a, e, i, o, u*).
- Look for key words in the sentence that may trigger a response.

Strategies for Essay Questions

Most students look at essay questions with dismay because they take more time. Yet essay tests can be one of the easiest tests to take because they give you a chance to show what you really know. An essay question requires you to supply the information. If you have studied, you will find that once you begin to answer an essay question, your answer will flow more easily. Some tips for answering essay questions are the following:

- More is not always better; sometimes more is just more. Try to be as concise and informative as possible. An instructor would rather see one page of excellent material than five pages of fluff.

from ordinary to Extraordinary

H.P. Rama, CEO, JHM Hotels, Greenville, SC

H.P. Rama has led an extraordinary life because he made it happen! Born in Africa, he was sent to India to live with his grandparents and to go to school when he was just five years old. He lived away from his parents in a little farming village in India where he finished school and ultimately earned an undergraduate degree. He knew he wanted to come to America and pursue the "American Dream," so when he was 21, he arrived in New York City with $2 in his pocket.

> At the age of 21, he left India and arrived in this country with $2 in his pocket.

He quit his first job as a dishwasher in just four hours and quickly moved onto his next job as a waiter at a Howard Johnson's restaurant in Manhattan. While he worked as a waiter to support himself, he attended Xavier University to pursue his MBA. H.P.'s life was primarily one of work and sacrifice as he worked hard to pay his expenses and to graduate with the degree he prized so much. Although H.P. had intended to become a banker, he and his brother had an opportunity to buy a hotel in California, so he jumped at the chance. He and his brother worked 24/7 doing every job required to run the hotel. In 1983, he bought four Howard Johnson hotels—just 13 years after working there as a waiter. Ultimately, H.P. and his family owned and developed 78 hotels, and still own 38 today.

He and his brothers developed a five-star hotel in India in 1990, and today are expanding and adding other hotels. H.P. is using knowledge learned in this wonderful country to continue the dream in India. To show appreciation for his great fortune in America, H.P. donated $1 million to the American Motel and Hotel Lodging Association to be used for college scholarships for hospitality students. He moved from ordinary to extraordinary!

EXTRAORDINARY REFLECTION

Mr. Rama worked his way up the ladder and became Chairman of the American Motel and Hotel Lodging Association, a major organization. What top honors do you hope to achieve in your own career? Why? How would they change your life?

■ Pay close attention to the action word used in the question and respond with the appropriate type of answer. Key words used in questions include the following:

discuss	illustrate	enumerate	describe
compare	define	relate	list
contrast	summarize	analyze	explain
trace	evaluate	critique	interpret
diagram	argue	justify	prove

■ Write a thesis statement for each answer.

■ Outline your thoughts before you begin to write.

■ Watch your spelling, grammar, and punctuation. Write neatly.

■ Use details, such as times, dates, places, and proper names, where appropriate.

■ Be sure to answer all parts of the question; some discussion questions have more than one part.

■ Summarize your main ideas toward the end of your answer.

■ Proofread your answer.

REFLECTIONS
on Studying and Test Taking

Just as reading is a learned skill, so are memory development, studying, and learning how to take assessments. You can improve your memory, but it will take practice, patience, and persistence. You can improve your study skills, but it will take time and work. And, you can increase your ability to do well on tests but it will take a commitment on your part to study smarter and put in the time and dedication required. By making the decision "*I Can Do This,*" you've won the battle; for when you make that decision, your studying and learning becomes easier.

Knowledge in Bloom

REDUCING TEST ANXIETY

Each lesson-end assessment is based on Bloom's Taxonomy of Learning. See the first page of this lesson for a quick review.

This activity uses levels 2–6 of the taxonomy

Explanation: Below, you will find listed six of the common physical or mental symptoms of anxiety reported by students while testing. **Process:** Beside each symptom, *create* *a list* of at least two concrete, doable, realistic strategies to overcome this physical or emotional anxiety symptom before or during a testing situation.

SYMPTOM	HOW TO REDUCE IT
Fatigue	1.
	2.
Frustration	1.
	2.
Fear	1.
	2.
Anger	1.
	2.
Nervousness/Nausea	1.
	2.
Uncertainty/Doubt	1.
	2.

REFERENCES

McCornack, S. (2007). *Reflect and Relate: An Introduction to Interpersonal Communication.* Boston: Bedford-St. Martin's Press.

Monaghan, P. (2009). *The Goddess Path: Myths, Invocations, and Rituals.* Woodbury, MN: Llewellyn Publications.

Woolfolk, A. (2006). *Educational Psychology* (10th ed.). Boston: Allyn and Bacon.

lesson nine
COMMUNICATION AND DIVERSITY

IMPROVING COMMUNICATION, CELEBRATING DIVERSITY, AND MANAGING CONFLICTS

Shutterstock

"Words can destroy relationships. What we call each other ultimately becomes what we think about each other, and what we think about each other matters."
—Jeanne J. Kirkpatrick

Why read this lesson?

Because you'll learn how to:

- Recommend strategies to appropriately communicate with diverse audiences, including peers, instructors, and teams

Because you'll be able to:

- Explain how to adjust your communication to suit your audience
- Recommend best practices for forming and participating in teams
- Explain ways to manage conflict in one-on-one and team settings

Knowledge in Bloom

Bloom's Taxonomy of Learning is a simple way of explaining the levels at which we all learn material and acquire information. The learning levels progress from basic to more complex learning and thinking. Examples are detailed below. Throughout this lesson, you'll see colorful triangles to the side of some activities. They let you know on which level of Bloom's Taxonomy the questions are based.

- **LEVEL 1: Remember**
  Describe the three communication goals.
- **LEVEL 2: Understand**
  Explain computer-mediated communication.
- **LEVEL 3: Apply**
  Sketch the design for the verb, "Conflict."
- **LEVEL 4: Analyze**
  Outline the steps in building and working with teams.
- **LEVEL 5: Evaluate**
  In one paragraph, predict what would happen without communication in your life.
- **LEVEL 6: Create**
  Propose a way to solve a conflict.

MyStudentSuccessLab

MyStudentSuccessLab is an online solution designed to help you acquire and develop (or hone) the skills you need to succeed. You will have access to peer-led video presentations and develop core skills through interactive exercises and projects.

THE COMMUNICATION PROCESS

How Does Communication Work and How Do We Communicate with Diverse Audiences?

Look around any store, at any red light, in any restaurant, and, often, in any classroom, and you will see someone on a cell phone. Increasingly, they are not talking, rather texting. Technology is one of the dominant forms of communication in today's world. Does texting count as communication? You bet it does. Does talking on a phone or writing an e-mail count as communication? Yes, it does. Does public speaking count as communication? Yes, it does, too. We are living in a world where communication and technology merge every day. This lesson is included to help you understand face-to-face communication, technological communication, communicating more effectively, how to appreciate the diverse nature of your audiences, and how to manage the inevitable conflicts that arise from time to time.

Communication is not something we do **to people**, rather it is something that is done **between people**. Communication can take on a variety of forms, such as oral speech, the written word, body movements, electronic messages, and even yawns. All of these actions communicate something to another person. As you begin thinking about communication, it is paramount that you know this: If you are in the presence of another person, just *one person*, communication cannot be stopped even if talking is not taking place.

> *"I see communication as a huge umbrella that covers and affects all that goes on between human beings."*
> —Joseph Adler

What Is the Role of Communication in Everyday Life?

Communication is a continuum between two (or more) people in which the messages exchanged significantly influence thoughts, emotions, behaviors, and relationships (McCornack, 2007). Oral communication is not static like the words in a book, a written letter, or a text message; it is fluid and constantly changing, potentially causing your relationships to change. Texting and e-mails are components of communication, as well as computer-mediated communication, which we will discuss later in this lesson.

In his book, *Reflect and Relate* (2007), Steven McCornack suggests that there are three communication goals, as shown in Figure 9.1. They are: **self-presentation goals, instrumental goals**, and **relationship goals**.

Level 3 Apply

Take a moment and review the communication goals in Figure 9.1. Then, identify one way that you could use each of the communication goals to help you succeed in college and establish strong relationships.

Self-Presentation Goal

I can use this to _____

_____

_____

Instrumental Goal

I can use this to _____

_____

_____

Relationship Goal

I can use this to _____

_____

_____

Figure 9.1   **Discovering Your Reading Style**

TYPE OF GOAL	EXPLANATION	EXAMPLE
Self-Presentation Goals	Goals that help us present ourselves to others in a particular fashion and help others see us as we wish to be seen	If you want a new acquaintance or love interest to see you as a caring, compassionate person, you will use words and actions that reveal yourself as caring, trustworthy, honest, and compassionate.
Instrumental Goals	Goals that help us present information in a way so that we get what we want or need from another person; to possibly win approval	If you wanted to borrow your best friend's laptop, you would remind him or her that you are always careful and respect others' property.
Relationship Goals	Goals that help us build meaningful, lasting, and effective relationships with other people	If your friend loaned you his or her computer, you might write a thank you note or buy a small gift to show your gratitude.

O M G U R O T T (OH MY GOD, YOU ARE OVER THE TOP)

Why Is Studying Computer-Mediated Communication Important in Today's Society?

"The information superhighway is clearly not just a road for moving data from one place to another, but a roadside where people can pass each other, occasionally meet, and decide to travel together."

—Beebe, Beebe, and Redmond (2008)

Believe it or not, there was a time not too long ago when there was no such term as *computer-mediated communication* (CMC). There were no e-mails, Blackberries, iPhones, tablets, text messages, blogs, tweets, Facebook pages, or instant messages. OMG, YKM! No, we're not kidding you. As a matter of fact, it was not until a few years ago that the study of communication even mentioned CMC. It was not considered to be a part of the communication process.

Today, CMC is a vital sub-category of the communication process. "There is some evidence that those wishing to communicate a message to someone, such as a message ending a relationship, may select a less-rich communication message—they may be more likely to send a letter or an e-mail rather than share the bad news face-to-face" (Beebe, Beebe, & Redmond, 2008). Technology has become an integral part of our communication strategies.

Some may ask, Can CMC really be considered "communication" when you are not meeting face-to-face with another person? The answer is yes. Why? Because in today's rich CMC environment, we can ***infer or imply emotions*** as we send and receive electronic communication. For example, we use symbols such as ☺ to indicate happiness or funny and ☹ to indicate sad or upset. We use abbreviations such as LOL (for "laugh out loud"). We even SCREAM AT OTHERS or SPEAK WITH EMPHASIS when we use all capital letters in our communication. Additionally, many people have cameras connected to their computers, and the sender and receiver can see each other's facial expressions on the screen. Therefore, emotions can be conveyed through CMC although there are not as many nonverbal clues to view and interpret as in face-to-face communication (Lane, 2008). Because we cannot see all the nonverbal clues associated with face-to-face communications, we are more likely to misunderstand the message when using CMC.

How much time do you spend online? Is it a wise use of your time?
Fotolia

The fact that we are not face-to-face does not seem to negatively affect our communication efforts via technology. Several studies suggest that CMC relationships differ very little from those who meet face-to-face. Further research also suggests that CMC relationships may even be stronger than face-to-face relationships because people using CMC ask more pointed and direct questions, reveal more about themselves, and communicate more frequently (Tidwell & Walther, 2002; Walther & Burgoon, 1992). Think about the last time you revealed something online that you may have never revealed to that person face-to-face.

There can be a downside and some challenges to CMC, however. For years, communication experts have worried about the effects of electronic communication on the entire communication process. In today's technologically advanced world, we do not have to speak to anyone if we don't want to. We purchase gasoline at the pump, pay for groceries at self-checkout, use automated tellers to get money, go to Amazon or iTunes to purchase our music and books, search eBay for sale items, and text others rather than pick up the phone or visit someone. Social isolation is a major concern and you have to work hard to guard against becoming ***emotionally detached*** and ***technologically reclusive***.

ADJUSTING YOUR COMMUNICATION STYLE TO SUIT YOUR AUDIENCE

Does It Really Matter?

It is advisable that you consider how you want to deliver a message. The old saying, "one size fits all" does not apply to the communication process. You will need to give careful consideration to the message, the receiver, and the channel. You will need to take into consideration the barriers that may occur based on how you deliver your message. You may have the same message to deliver to several people. It may be best to e-mail John the message, but this channel will not work with Miriam. It may be best to have a face-to-face meeting with Seng, but a text will work with Kayla. Basically, you have to ask yourself, do I want to say "*I love you*" via Facebook or in person? Would I rather hear "*I'm sorry*" over the phone or in an e-mail? Would I approach my instructor about an extension for a project in person or with a text message? These are decisions faced by today's communicators.

When deciding which communication channel to use, consider Figure 9.2 for the timeline of delivery, richness of your message, and control over the outcome.

Figure 9.2 Choosing Your Communication Path

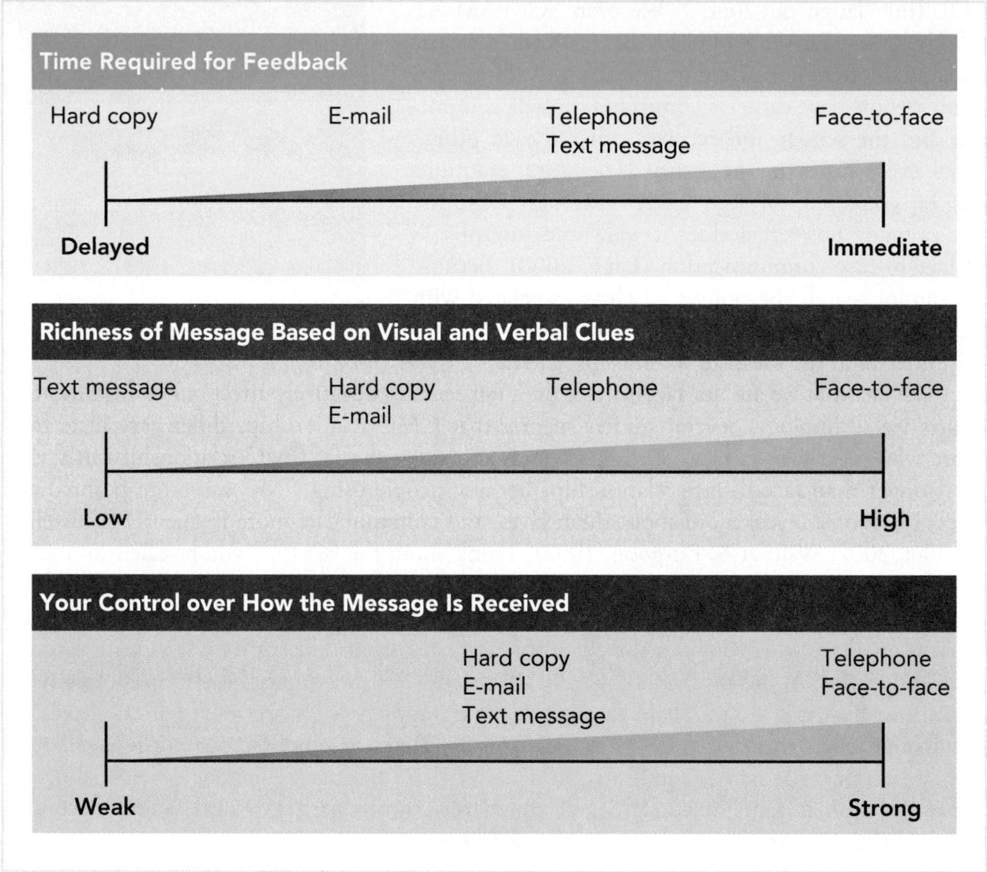

Time Required for Feedback

| Hard copy | E-mail | Telephone Text message | Face-to-face |

Delayed   Immediate

Richness of Message Based on Visual and Verbal Clues

| Text message | Hard copy E-mail | Telephone | Face-to-face |

Low   High

Your Control over How the Message Is Received

| Hard copy E-mail Text message | Telephone Face-to-face |

Weak   Strong

Source: Based on Adler, Rosenfeld, and Proctor (2010).

COMMUNICATING IN VARIOUS SITUATIONS

How Are Supportive Teams Built?

Is teamwork really important? I love to work on my own, why do I need a team? Won't I get distracted if I'm around other people? These may be some of the thoughts you have about working in teams. The simple truth is this: Yes, you may work best alone and you may not value teamwork at the moment, however, you may not have a choice while at school or in your career.

Some people think of teamwork as just a bunch of people getting together. In actuality teamwork is when a group of people make a deliberate effort to work together to achieve a common goal by a certain date. It involves a common approach, a shared attitude for success, and trust in others on the team.

Teams can be extremely valuable to your academic studies, in your personal life, and in your professional career as well. Some of the benefits of teamwork include:

- Learning from others' ideas
- Being able to bounce ideas off others
- Being able to share the workload
- Being able to draw from others' experiences
- Being able to draw on the talents and skills brought together in one space and time
- Being able to trust, rely upon, and call on one another

Sometimes, teams do not work. It can be because of interpersonal issues, outside conflicts, unclear goals, or no timeline. In the book, *The Five Dysfunctions of a Team* (2002), author Patrick Lencioni discusses why teams fail and how to recognize the symptoms. The five dysfunctions include:

- Lack of trust
- Excessive conflict
- Lack of commitment
- Little or no accountability
- Failure to focus on results

How will learning to work on a team help you in your career?
Shutterstock

As you begin to build, communicate, and work in teams, you will want to think about the following questions:

- What are the objectives and timeline of the team?
- What is the benefit from working in a team versus working alone?
- What resources will be needed to accomplish the goal and how does the team get them?
- What information will be needed to ensure the team's success?
- What are the personalities of each team member? Will they mesh?
- Do the team members have a personal agenda? If so, how will this be addressed?
- Do the members have a collaborative spirit?
- Does each person have something to bring to the team?
- How will the team know when it has reached its goal?

Guidelines for Setting Up an Effective Team

Consider these guidelines as you begin working with your team:

- Decide on a meeting place.
- Try to create a comfortable, engaging, and fun atmosphere.
- Establish an environment where everyone can share and contribute.
- If possible, limit the number of members on the team to 5–7.
- Have a goal and a timeline for completion.
- Make sure each team member is working toward the same goal.
- Communicate as often as possible, depending on the needs of the team.
- Ensure that everyone has a role—note taking, researching, surveying, etc.
- Ensure that all team members do their assigned tasks so that all can benefit.

from ordinary to Extraordinary

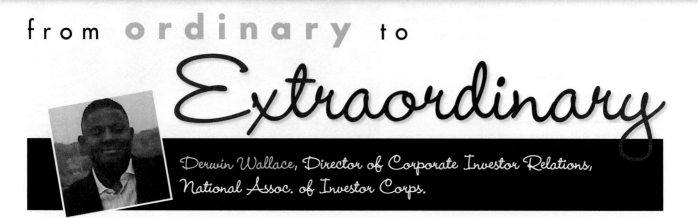

Derwin Wallace, Director of Corporate Investor Relations, National Assoc. of Investor Corps.

Derwin was born in a ghetto on the West Side of Chicago. His father was a strict man from the Mississippi Delta and his way of disciplining his children was to beat them—Derwin included. By the sixth grade, Derwin had a job, paid rent, and bought his own school lunches and clothes. When he was 16, he had saved enough money to buy a boom box. One night he was playing the boom box, and because it was plugged into an electrical outlet, using power and increasing electrical costs, his father took the power cord and began to beat him with it. It was at this point that he knew he had to leave . . . and leave he did.

Derwin broke into a friend's garage and wrapped himself in blankets and paper to keep from freezing to death. Later, he hid in his basement and was nearly eaten to death by rats. He began to stop by an old bakery to get their thrown-away donuts to feed the rats so they would leave him alone. That is how he survived. He went on to live in busses and abandoned buildings and cars. He was on the high school tennis team and diving team, so he had a key to the school gym. He took showers in the locker room. He lived like this for two years. After high school graduation, others went out to party and Derwin found himself celebrating in an abandoned car.

After high school, he joined the military for a few years and was asked to leave due to acts of immaturity. After the military, he began his college studies, but dropped out shortly thereafter because of money and many other life situations. His life was going nowhere. He lived in rented rooms for eight years. One day, Derwin decided to move to Atlanta and found himself homeless again. He began work as a telemarketer and found another room to rent. At 28, he found himself with nothing. He had a dead-end job, no

■ Ensure that all members give and receive effective, constructive feedback.
■ Have fun and celebrate together.

How Can I Strengthen My Relationship with People of Diverse Backgrounds?

We've talked about the rule of communication, suggesting that if you are in the presence of another person, *you are communicating*. It is inescapable. Well, it is also inescapable that we all live in a diverse world with people from different socio-economic, cultural, religious, and ideological backgrounds. The American culture is one of the most diverse of any on Earth! We are a nation of immigrants that still welcomes people from all over the world to our shores.

What Are the Dimensions of Diversity?

Among the kinds of diversity you might encounter are race, religion, gender, age, ethnicity, nationality, culture, sexual orientation, social class, geographic region, and physical challenges. It is important for you to become open to individuals in all dimensions of diversity. The most

education, and was dating a woman who was, unknown to him, an occasional drug user. Something had to change. His life had to change. He looked around at others and wondered why they had a nice life and he did not. Finally, he realized that he had to look at his own life and actions before he could blame anyone else. He decided his lack of education was holding him back.

Derwin had seen an ad for DeVry University and he decided to investigate. He had been interested in math and accounting. He decided to enroll and was able to get tutoring and individual attention in the small classes. Some of his instructors worked in the accounting and investment field and shared their real-world experiences. After his first semester, he had a 4.0 GPA and received a Georgia Lottery Scholarship. He made the Dean's List and was a President's Scholar.

Because of his accounting and business classes, he began to watch the stock market. As crazy as it seems, he took the extra money from his loans and scholarships and began to invest it in stocks. After six years, he graduated with a B.S. in Accounting and an MBA concentration in

> *Derwin broke into a friend's garage and wrapped himself in blankets and paper to keep from freezing to death. Later, he hid in his basement and was nearly eaten to death by rats.*

Finance. His education assisted him in obtaining careers as a stock broker, financial analyst, investor relations professional, and financial controller. As Director of Corporate Investor Relations, Derwin's main responsibility is to put companies that trade in the stock market in front of investors in hopes they may purchase that companies stock.

Education took Derwin from living homeless in a rat-infested basement to flying in corporate jets and working with some of the most wealthy and powerful companies in America. His education gave him limitless opportunities. He has often stated that "corporate America is a battlefield and you must get your armor ready. Your education is your preparation for battle—it is your boot camp for the real world." Derwin learned this lesson and moved from ordinary to extraordinary!

EXTRAORDINARY REFLECTION

What role has your family played in shaping your experiences and future? How can you use this to your best advantage?

significant thing you can do is to think of people who have more diverse backgrounds than you as individuals, not as groups. Some of you will need to make bigger changes in your overall belief system than others; it all depends on what kind of background you came from and what experiences you have had.

CONFLICT IN RELATIONSHIPS IS INEVITABLE

Why Is It Important to Learn How You Deal with Conflict in One-on-One and Team Situations?

Many people intensely dislike conflict and will go to extreme measures to avoid it, whether it is one-on-one or with a group of people. On the other hand, some people seem to thrive on conflict and enjoy creating situations that put people at odds with each other. While in school, you certainly will not be sheltered from conflicts. The simple truth is conflict is pervasive throughout our culture, and you simply cannot avoid having some confrontations with other people.

Figure 9.3 **Chinese Figure for Conflict**

Danger   Hidden Opportunity

Therefore, you should not try to avoid conflict; rather, you can use it to create better relationships by exploring workable solutions—hopefully win-win solutions.

Consider the Chinese symbol for *conflict* in Figure 9.3. You will see that it is made up of two different symbols: **Danger** and **Hidden Opportunity**. Why? Because when you are engaged in a conflict, you have the potential to enter into ***dangerous*** territory. Violence, alienation, and irreparable damage could be caused. However, you also have the ***hidden opportunity*** to grow, learn, and strengthen your relationships. Just because conflict in relationships is inevitable does not mean that it has to be permanent, dangerous, or destructive.

Conflict can occur in any relationship, whether it is with family members, your girlfriend or boyfriend, your best friend, a roommate, a spouse or partner, your children, or a total stranger.

Some of the causes of ***relationship tensions*** include:

Jealousy	Honesty	Emotions
Dependency	Culture	Sexual orientation
Outside commitments	Opinions/values/beliefs	Perceptions
Personality traits or flaws	Affiliations	

Dealing with Conflict

Conflict does not happen in just one form. Conflict can be personal or situational. There are several ways that people deal with issues. They include:

- **Blowing your lid**. This involves screaming, uncontrolled anger, hurling insults, and an unwillingness to listen.
- **Shunning**. This involves shutting the other person out and being unwilling to engage in any type of communication or resolution.
- **Sarcasm**. This involves using stinging remarks to make the other person feel small, unimportant, insignificant, or stupid.
- **Mocking**. This involves using past experiences or words to "mock" or ridicule the other person; laughing at them; poking fun at them or the situation.
- **Civility**. This involves sitting down and logically, rationally discussing the issues or problems and trying to come to a win-win solution. (Adapted from L. A. Baxter. 1993. Conflict Management: An Episodic Approach. *Small Group Behavior, 13*(1), 23–24.)

Dealing with Conflict in Everyday Situations

As much as we try to live a conflict-free life, it is impossible. Conflicts arise with strangers at the grocery store and with people we love and see every day. Conflict is simply a fact of life. However, you do not have to dwell on the conflict, you don't have to let the conflict ruin your day, and you don't always have to win. Consider the following important tips for dealing with conflicts that may arise in your life:

- Check your own behavior and language to determine if you caused or added to the conflict. If so, apologize and move on.
- Work hard to understand the cause of the conflict. Ask questions. Ask what the other person needs.
- Avoid physical contact with others at every expense. This can only lead to more trouble, pain, and heartache (and sometimes money if you're arrested).
- Try to create a "win/win" situation where everyone can walk away having gained something.
- Allow the other person to "save face." Give the other person a way out—a way to avoid embarrassment and pain.

REFLECTIONS
on Communication, Diversity, and Conflict Management

Few tools will ever give you the power to affect change more than effective communication skills. By working to improve your communication skills, your appreciation of diversity, and your conflict management abilities, you will begin to see how the relationships in your life begin to change and improve.

Knowledge
in Bloom

BUILDING A TEAM AND SOLVING A PROBLEM

Each lesson-end assessment is based on Bloom's Taxonomy of Learning. See the first page of this lesson for a quick review.

This activity uses levels 1–6 of the taxonomy

DIRECTIONS: Using the information from this lesson and research that you may have found online or in print, develop a Ten-Point Plan to establish an **online** (virtual) team that will work to solve the problem presented by your supervisor. Remember to consider the make-up of the team, the objectives, and the intended outcomes.

SITUATION: You work for an international company. Your supervisor has asked you to lead a virtual team comprised of members of your company from across the world. You know that your supervisor is expecting you to be successful in this endeavor and solve the problem at hand. Your next promotion hinges on your work with this team. What steps would you take to begin the team-building process, invite members, approach the problem, solicit solutions, research ideas, decide on a solution, present your findings and recommendations, and reward the team members? Your Ten-Point Plan should be detailed and effective.

REFERENCES

Adler, R., Rosenfeld, L., & Proctor, R. (2010). *Interplay: The Process of Interpersonal Communication* (11th ed.). New York, NY: Oxford University Press.

Baxter, L. A. (1993). Conflict management: An episodic approach. *Small Group Behavior, 13*(1), 23–24.

Beebe, S., & Redmond, M. (2008). *Interpersonal Communication: Relating to Others* 95th Boston: Allyn and Bacon.

Lane, H. (1976). *The Wild Boy of Aveyron.* Cambridge, MA: Harvard University Press.

Lencioni, P. (2002). *The Five Dysfunctions of a Team: A Leadership Fable.* San Francisco: Jossey-Bass.

McCornack, S. (2007). *Reflect and Relate: An Introduction to Interpersonal Communication.* Boston: Bedford-St. Martin's Press.

Tidwell, L., & Walther, J. (2002). Computer-mediated communication effects on disclosure, impressions, and interpersonal evaluations: Getting to know one another a bit at a time. *Human Communication Research, 28*, 317–348.

Walther, J., & Burgoon, J. (1992). Relational communication in computer-mediated interaction. *Human Communication Research, 19*, 50–88.

INFORMATION LITERACY

DETERMINING THE CREDIBILITY OF IDEAS AND RESOURCES

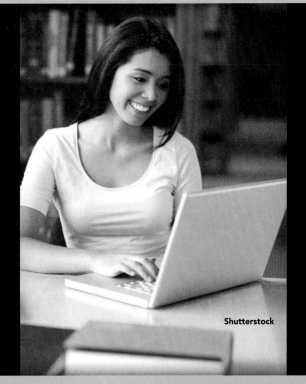

Shutterstock

"More information, by overwhelming and distracting the brain, can make it harder to tap into just the core information you need." —Eric Kessler

INFORMATION LITERACY

Why read this lesson?

Because you'll learn how to:

- Evaluate sources for reliability, credibility, currency, and accuracy

Because you'll be able to:

- Explain information literacy
- Describe strategies for finding appropriate information sources
- Explain what makes a source reliable, credible, current, and accurate
- Explain how to use sources ethically

Knowledge in Bloom

Bloom's Taxonomy of Learning is a simple way of explaining the levels at which we all learn material and acquire information. The learning levels progress from basic to more complex learning and thinking. Examples are detailed below. Throughout this lesson, you'll see colorful triangles to the side of some activities. They let you know on which level of Bloom's Taxonomy the questions are based.

- **LEVEL 1: Remember**
  Define information literacy.
- **LEVEL 2: Understand**
  Explain each step in the D.A.R.T.S. Information Literacy System.
- **LEVEL 3: Apply**
  Apply the D.A.R.T.S. system to current research.
- **LEVEL 4: Analyze**
  Outline the steps in narrowing a topic.
- **LEVEL 5: Evaluate**
  Recommend appropriate sources for personal research.
- **LEVEL 6: Create**
  Write a detailed, critical review of an article.

MyStudentSuccessLab

MyStudentSuccessLab is an online solution designed to help you acquire and develop (or hone) the skills you need to succeed. You will have access to peer-led video presentations and develop core skills through interactive exercises and projects.

PRACTICING INFORMATION LITERACY IN THE AGE OF TECHNOLOGY

Why Is It Important to Know How to Sort Through and Evaluate Information?

Anyone, yes **anyone**, can post information on the Internet. Much of the information online is not screened for accuracy, judged on truth, or critiqued for its worth. Often, much of what you find online may not even indicate an author's name. Some of it will be accurate and valuable, while other pieces will be full of half-truths, downright lies, and false claims. Some information will be legitimate and helpful, and some will be nothing more than a false advertisement to con you into buying something or believing something. Some will be unbiased and impartial, and some will be slanted and unbalanced by the person or company by which it was posted. Therefore, it is up to you to learn how to determine the worth, value, credibility, and accuracy of the information you find online—and in print resources.

"Information literacy forms the basis of lifelong learning. It is common to all disciplines, to all learning environments, and to all levels of education."
—Association of Research Libraries

Information literacy (IL) includes the skills a person needs to determine what information is needed, where to find it, how much of it you need for a specific topic, how to analyze and organize it to create your "product," and, finally, how to properly cite it. The procedure is that simple and that complex. Information literacy impacts all aspects of your college career and will later play a major role in your success in the workplace. You will use information literacy when you write a paper, read an article and evaluate it, listen to presenters and determine if you believe what they are saying, and when preparing and making your own presentations. Information literacy is the cornerstone of an educated mind.

If you master the processes of information literacy, you will gain more control over what you are learning and how you can apply it. You will become more adept at distinguishing facts from untruths while selecting points that support your topic or research problem. Regardless of your major, you cannot escape the need to locate, analyze, apply, and present information in a compelling and logical manner. You will also become a more savvy consumer because you can make informed decisions about shopping, voting, investing, purchasing a home or car, choosing your major, and a host of other important life decisions.

THE INFORMATION LITERACY PROCESS

Can You Hit the Bull's Eye Using D.A.R.T.S.?

Becoming information literate does not just happen by opening a book or logging onto Google. True information literacy begins by understanding the process of research. This section will help you identify and remember the steps in using IL skills. Using the **D.A.R.T.S. Information**

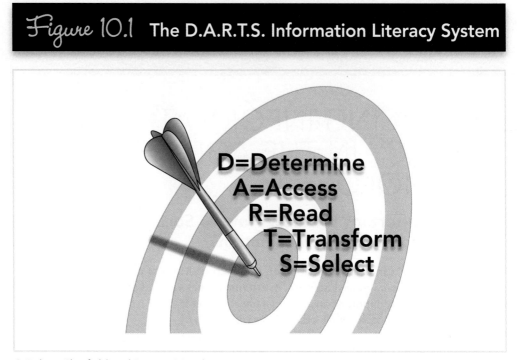

Figure 10.1 The D.A.R.T.S. Information Literacy System

D=Determine
A=Access
R=Read
T=Transform
S=Select

© Robert Sherfield and Patricia Moody

Literacy System (Figure 10.1), you can easily remember the steps, use them often, and benefit from their practicality.

D = Determine the Information You Need by Narrowing Your Topic

Research begins by asking a question. Suppose that you have been assigned a paper or speech and the topic is up to you. You decided that you want to write or speak on Rosa Parks. You begin the research and type "Rosa Parks" into Google. You get 3,520,000 hits. This is just a few too many articles to read by Monday. However, if you begin with a question in mind, you can narrow your topic and determine what information you need early on.

After some thought, you decide that your research question will be, *"What was Rosa Park's role in the Civil Rights Movement?"* If you Google this topic, you get 251,000 hits. Still far too many, but 3,269,000 fewer hits than before, *and*, you have a direction to begin your paper. So, the first step in becoming more information literate is to *identify and narrow your topic to determine what information is needed on this topic*. You will also need to determine what *type* of information you need and want to use in your project. Do you want facts, opinions, eyewitness reports, interviews, debates, and/or arguments? Each may provide you with different types of information.

> *"The booming science of decision making has shown that more information can lead to objectively poorer choices, and to choices that people come to regret."*
> —A. Dimoka

Cyber research can be an amazing tool in your educational pursuit. However, when you are faced with 3,520,000 articles on one topic, it can also become overwhelming. *Information overload* can have negative effects on the learning process. Angelika Dimoka, Director of The Center for Neural Decision Making at Temple University, suggests that with the vast amounts of information we face in an online search, "the brain's emotion region runs as wild as toddlers on a sugar high" (Begley, 2011). We begin to make stupid mistakes and bad decisions. Our frustration and anxiety levels also soar. Too much information can lead to *information paralysis*. This basically means that you have so much information that you don't know what to do with it so you do nothing.

The new field of decision making research also suggests that when people are faced with too much information and too many decisions, we tend to make no decision at all. When the amount of information coming at us is coupled with the *speed* at which it comes, this can lead to devastating results. According to Sharon Begley in her article, *I Can't Think* (2011), when faced with too much information, "we sacrifice accuracy and thoughtfulness to the false god of immediacy." We tend to make quick, bad decisions rather than slower, well-reasoned ones. It is for these reasons that step one in the D.A.R.T.S. Information Literacy System is imperative. When determining what information is needed on your narrowed topic, you should also make sure that you do the following:

- Understand your instructor's guidelines for the project
- Understand your intended audience
- Determine the availability of reliable resources and how many are required by your instructor
- Develop a timeline to complete your project.

A = Access the Appropriate Information from a Variety of Sources

After you have made your topic decision and narrowed your research question, you will want to begin the process of accessing valuable, reliable, credible information. While Wikipedia and Google are valuable tools, it is also important to use a variety of sources, such as journals, scholarly books, newspapers, and maybe even interviews, to gather the information needed.

You may be asking, *"Is the library still important in the Digital Age?"* Yes! The answer is an absolute yes! Many people think a library as a place that is quiet as a tomb with a crabby old librarian presiding over it who is prepared to pounce on you if you ask a question or touch one of her precious books. Fortunately, that stereotype went the way of the horse and buggy, and today, libraries are literally the hub of a college campus. Your library is a key you can use to unlock your education and help you become more information literate by accessing a variety of sources. Although the Internet is an amazing tool, serious research requires you to use the library and its tools, including print books, maps, charts, government data, periodicals, and your librarian. It may be fun and easy to Google, Dogpile, or Wikipedize, but you will also need to hone your library research skills and critical thinking abilities.

> "We are drowning in information and starving for wisdom."
> —E.O. Wilson

Some of the things that your librarian can assist you with include helping you discover, understand, search, and use the online catalog; narrow your digital search to get to the information you need; search other libraries for information and sources not available at your institution; discover, use, and evaluate databases for almost every subject area; and make use of interlibrary loan tools. They can also help you understand your own library's online data search systems.

How Can I Find Specific Information?

Often, you may need to find specific information. Perhaps you need to find a map of a specific country for your business management course, or you need to know if a book is in print, or the population of Iowa. Figure 10.2 can help you save a great deal of time. Remember, it is always best to view a number of resources (online and in print) to ensure the accuracy and validity of your information.

Figure 10.2 Information Made Easy

IF YOU NEED TO FIND . . .	SEARCH THESE ADDRESSES
How to locate a place or view a map	www.googleearth.com www.mapserve.maptech.com www.about.com
How to find if a book is in print	www.amazon.com Your college's library and librarian
U.S. and state population, economic, and workforce data	www.census.gov
Information on famous people (biographies)	www.loc.gov (loc=Library of Congress) www.who2.com www.biography.com/search
Unbiased information and comparisons on world religions	www.patheos.com
Federal or state legislation	www.thomas.loc.gov www.house.gov *www.whpgs.org/f.htm*
Magazine and newspaper articles	www.newslink.org www.infotrac.net www.ehow.com
Information about a specific country	www.infoplease.com www.countryreports.org
Information about careers	www.bls.gov www.careeroverview.com www.occupationalinfo.org
Brief contents and entire scanned books	www.books.google.com www.openlibrary.org
Simple, effective instructional videos on algebra, math, calculus, history, banking, finance, art history, civics, and more.	www.kahnacademy.org

Becoming information literate requires you to seek and use a variety of sources; however, you must also determine how much is enough. You don't want to overwhelm yourself. When searching for your resources, keep the following tips in mind:

- Understand that information comes in a variety of media, such as government documents, maps, videos, books, scholarly journals, online databases, and YouTube interviews, just to name a few.

- As you begin to put your information together to create your project, determine what information is missing and where you might locate it. You will also need to determine if you have too much information on a particular aspect of your topic.

- Manage your information carefully so that you know exactly where you found it. This will allow you to access the information later if needed, and allow you to provide proper citations once your project is complete.

Level 5 Evaluate

Now it is your turn. Consider that you have been asked to write a paper on "*The Value of a College Education.*" First, develop a brief thesis for your paper, and then find at least three online resources to help you write this paper. For this exercise, **do not** use Wikipedia.

THESIS: _____

_____

_____

Source #1: _____

Citation: _____

Why is this source suitable to your work? _____

_____

_____

Source #2: _____

Citation: _____

Why is this source suitable to your work? _____

_____

_____

Source #3: _____

Citation: _____

Why is this source suitable to your work? _____

_____

_____

R = Read and Evaluate the Information for Reliability, Credibility, and Accuracy

You have chosen your topic, narrowed it into a workable thesis, and found a variety of sources that you can use for your project. Let's say that you have found three Internet articles, one book, one YouTube video, and one journal article. It is now time to view and read your material in great detail and evaluate the information to determine if it is valid, accurate, and credible. Basically, you are working to discover if your sources present facts correctly and if the information is up-to-date, logical, fair, unbiased, and useable. By using the *Credibility Checklist* in Figure 10.3, you will have a better understanding of the quality of your information.

T = Transform the Information to Create Your Project

Now that you have found your information and evaluated its credibility and usefulness, it is time to actually *use* what you have found. It is time to transform these facts, figures, interviews, charts, graphs, and/or opinions into your project. You will need to determine what type of organizational pattern best suits your information. This may have been set by your instructor's guidelines. Organizing the body of your paper or speech can be done using one of several proven methods:

- **Spatial organization** is when you arrange information or items according to their direction or location.

Figure 10.3 What Makes a Source Reliable, Credible, Current, and Accurate?

Are the information and author credible, valid, accurate, and reliable?	■ Who is the author and what are his or her credentials, educational background, past writings, or experience? ■ From What edition is the source? Second and third editions suggest that the source has been updated to reflect changes and new knowledge. ■ Who is the publisher? If the source is published by a university press, it is likely to be a scholarly publication. ■ Does the information appear to be valid and well researched, or does it just gloss over the material? Is it supported by evidence and documentation? ■ What are the author's credentials? Anyone can put anything on the web. Your task is to distinguish between the reliable and questionable, the knowledgeable and the amateur.
Is the article fact or opinion, popular or scholarly?	■ What is the title of the source? This will help you determine if the source is popular, sensational, or scholarly, and indicates the level of complexity. Popular journals are resources such as *Time, Newsweek, Vogue, Ebony,* and *Reader's Digest.* They seldom cite their sources. Sensational resources are often inflammatory and written on an elementary level. They usually have flashy headlines, and they cater to popular superstitions. Examples are *The Globe, The National Enquirer,* and *The Star.* ■ Is the source factually objective, is it opinionated, or is it propaganda? Objective sources look at all angles and report on each one honestly. ■ Are sources documented with footnotes or links? In scholarly works, the credibility of most writings is proven through the footnote or endnote documentation.
Is it up to date and timely?	■ When was the source published? If it is a webpage, the date is usually found on the last page or the home page. Is the source current or out of date for your topic? ■ Look for the date that the article was last updated. Is the page dated? Is it current enough for your research or is it "stale" and outdated?
Does it have depth?	■ What is the intended audience of your source? Is the information too simple, too advanced, or too technical for your audience?
Is it logical?	■ Could the article be parody, humor, or satire? ■ Ask yourself, "Why was this page put on the web?"
Is it fair?	■ Does the article present both sides of the argument? Is it balanced? ■ Was the article written by a neutral source on the topic?
Are the sources of the information cited? Does it include a bibliography?	■ Does the writer of the book, article, or website cite his or her sources? If not, what does this mean for the credibility of the information?

Source: Adapted from Ormondroyd, Engle, and Cosgrave (2001) and UC-Berkeley (2005).

- **Cause–effect organization** is when you arrange your information in the cause-and-effect order. You would discuss the causes of a problem and then explore its effects.

- **Chronological organization** is presenting information in the order in which it happened. Topics that deal with historical facts and how-to papers often use chronological organization.

- **Problem-solving organization** is often used in persuasive papers. Usually, you are trying to get your reader to accept your proposal. You first begin by pointing out the major problem(s), and then move on to revealing the solutions, and the advantages of the solutions.

- **Topical/categorical organization** is when you group information into subdivisions or cluster information into categories. Some information naturally falls into specific categories, such as the different types of palm trees or the types of roller skates available.

How can organizing your project in advance save you time?
Johnny Lye/iStockphoto

- **Compare/contrast organization** is when you present your information in a fashion that shows its similarities to and differences from other information.

- **Importance/priority organization** allows you to arrange information from the most important issue to the least, or the least important to the most important. You can also arrange your information from the top priority to the lowest priority, or vice versa.

S = Select the Appropriate Documentation Style for Credibility and Ethics

You're not finished yet. Now, you must let your readers or listeners know where you located your information. This is called citation or documentation of your sources. You will need to document and cite all statistics, quotes, and excerpts from works that you referenced. To skip this step is an unethical and dangerous thing to do. Sure, you may not get caught, but the consequences of plagiarism are monumental—not to mention the residual damage to your ethics and credibility.

The most common means of doing this is by quoting within the paper and then compiling a reference or bibliography sheet at the end. If you have questions about what to document, consider the following by Kirszner and Mandell (1995). The following must be cited if used:

- *Any* copyrighted information (music, poems, literary works, films, photographs, videos, artwork, advertisements, plays, computer programs, or audio files, just to name a few); most of these works require that you seek permission to use them, and many require that you pay royalty to the author or his/her heirs

- Direct quotations

- Opinions, judgments, and insights of others that you summarize or paraphrase

- Information that is not widely known

- Information that is open to dispute

- Information that is not commonly accepted

- Tables, charts, graphs, and statistics taken from a source

There are several acceptable ways to document your research. The three most widely used methods are the **MLA** (Modern Language Association), the **APA** (American Psychological Association), and the **CMS** (Chicago Manual of Style). All three styles can be explained by your librarian, through the MLA, APA, or CMS style guides, and/or by searching online.

By using the D.A.R.T.S. Information Literacy System, you can rest assured that you are approaching the mountains of information in a more organized and reasonable fashion. These simple steps can mean the difference between information overload and information mastered.

from **ordinary** to

Extraordinary

Matthew L. Karres, Motivational Speaker/Team Leader, Weight Watchers International

"Fatso!" The word still rings in Matt's ears 40 years after she yelled it. When Matt was four years old and in pre-school, he rode a bus to school and he was the second person to be picked up. One student was already on the bus. When he climbed the steps and took his seat that first day, she yelled that word, "Fatso," and thus began the years of verbal and emotional abuse.

He had always been big for his age. He had to have a larger desk than "normal" from kindergarten onward. By his eighth birthday, Matt weighed about 120 pounds and stood 5'9" tall. By the time he was in the sixth grade, he was 6'2" tall and even heavier. So there he was, tall, overweight, shy, and introverted. In junior high, when he had to weigh in for gym class, his classmates would run over to see how much he weighed. The scale read 225 pounds. In the ninth grade, his weight had soared to 280 pounds, and he wore size 48 pants. This is when his mother first took him to Overeaters Anonymous. In the time period between the ninth and tenth grade, Matt lost 100 pounds by going on a very restricted diet. He was happy—or so he thought. His happiness was short-lived as the weight soon began rising again.

For the next eight years, he began to gain massive amounts of weight and the depression that followed was just as massive. His parents moved 3000 miles away, college was not going well, he was lonely, fat, depressed, and, to be truthful, suicidal. Food became his only friend—his best friend. In 10 years, he gained over 250 pounds, reaching nearly 500 pounds and wearing size 62 pants. He developed sleep apnea, heart problems, and limb numbness.

He had to try something drastic, so he applied to become one of the first candidates for weight loss surgery. He had the surgery, but was given very inadequate warnings about the side effects: throwing up, gas, withdrawal, *and* that it was not a miracle cure. However, over three years, Matt lost 300 pounds and had two reconstructive surgeries. Things were good. Again, this was short-lived. He started gaining weight again, and before he knew it, he had gained 100 pounds. He was in horrible despair. Hopelessness was all he felt. Matt's mom suggested that he join Weight Watchers. He told her that he had tried that before, and then she said the words that changed his life forever.

> Matt ate three Hostess fruit pies on the way to the Weight Watchers meeting.

"Matt," she stated. *"You have not tried Weight Watchers. You tried their program* **your** *way. You did not try their program* **their** *way."* He decided to re-join. He ate three Hostess Fruit Pies on the way to the Weight Watchers meeting.

This time, he surrendered—he gave in to **their** program. He did the mental and the physical work. Soon, he was losing weight again in a healthy and lasting fashion. He dropped down to 190 pounds. By learning to eat properly, exercise, and think about everything that he put into his mouth, he has now kept the weight steady for ten years. Now, Matt holds his "dream job" as a Motivational Leader for Weight Watchers. It has **not** been easy, and he states that he fights every day and that there is no bigger food addict than him. However, Matt learned to apply what he learned. He moved from ordinary to extraordinary!

EXTRAORDINARY REFLECTION

Matthew decided that he had to take a drastic measure (surgery in his case) to make a positive change in his life. What drastic changes might you have to make in your life to bring about positive change?

REFLECTIONS
on Information Literacy

Becoming information literate is the basis for your lifelong education. This skill will help you determine what information is needed, how to evaluate its worth, how to tell if it is current, and how to use the information to create something new. Knowing how to effectively research a topic can mean the difference between buying a car that is poorly rated to voting for a candidate that

stands against what you value. It can mean the difference between an investment that helps you retire, or a choice that bankrupts you. And, it can mean the difference between submitting a paper that is shallow and trivial, or a stunning paper that shows your ability, skills, and knowledge in the selection, evaluation, and use of information.

Knowledge in Bloom

BUILDING YOUR INFORMATION LITERACY SKILLS

Each lesson-end assessment is based on Bloom's Taxonomy of Learning. See the first page of this lesson for a quick review.

This activity uses levels 1–6 of the taxonomy

Directions: Find an in depth website or online article about a *major current event within the last month*. Using the information from the article and/or website, complete the

following Information Literacy Checklist and Worksheet. Justify your answers.

Event?

_____

Why is this event important?

_____

_____

_____

Name of website or online article:

_____

URL address of website or article:

_____

Publisher or affiliation:

_____

Publication date:

_____

Author:

_____

After reading the website or article, use other sources (books, journals, or other online sites) to compare/contrast your findings and to justify your responses.

QUESTION	YOUR RESPONSE		JUSTIFY YOUR RESPONSE
Is the author's name indicated?	Yes	No	Name?
Is the author of the source credible? Reliable?	Yes	No	Why?
Is the source from an individual web page, an organization, a government agency, a for-profit agency, an international source, a military site, or an educational institution?	Type:		How do you know?
Is this site easy to navigate, read, and use?	Yes	No	Why?
Does the author provide contact information or can you find the contact information online?	Yes	No	Contact information:
Is this source masked as an advertisement?	Yes	No	Justify.
Does this source require that you have or purchase special software or join a site to view portions of the material?	Yes	No	What is required? How much does it cost?
Did the source provide enough information to begin a project on this person? Does it offer an in-depth look at the topic?	Yes	No	List three important facts you gained from this source:
Is the information accurate?	Yes	No	Justify.
Is the article dated?	Yes	No	Date of publication?
Is the information current?	Yes	No	Justify.
Is the information objective and fair?	Yes	No	Justify.
Is the article an opinion piece or a factual piece?	Opinion	Fact	Justify.
Does the article provide both sides to the event?	Yes	No	Justify.
Does the article provide live links within the piece?	Yes	No	List the URL of one link:
Does the author provide footnotes and references for his/her research?	Yes	No	List one of his/her references used to write this piece:

REFERENCES

Begley, S. (2011, March 7). I can't think. *Newsweek*, pp. 28–33.

Kirszner L., & Mandell, S. (1995). *The Holt Handbook*. Orlando, FL: Harcourt Brace College Publishers.

Ormondroyd, J., Engle, M., & Cosgrave, T. (2001). *How to Critically Analyze Information Sources*. Ithaca, NY: Cornell University Libraries.

UC Berkeley Teaching Library Internet Workshop. (2005). Evaluating web pages: Techniques to apply and questions to ask. Retrieved from www.lib.berkeley.edu/TeachingLib/Guides?internet?Evaluate.hrt. Copyright by the Regents of the University of California.

lesson eleven

LIVE

DEALING WITH STRESS IN POSITIVE WAYS

"Adopting the right attitude can convert a negative stress into a positive one."
—Hans Selye

Why read this lesson?

Because you'll learn how to:

- Create a stress management plan

Because you'll be able to:

- Identify major stressors that affect students
- Identify personal stressors
- Analyze your reaction to personal stressors
- Recommend tips for managing stress

Knowledge in Bloom

Bloom's Taxonomy of Learning is a simple way of explaining the levels at which we all learn material and acquire information. The learning levels progress from basic to more complex learning and thinking. Examples are detailed below. Throughout this lesson, you'll see colorful triangles to the side of some activities. They let you know on which level of Bloom's Taxonomy the questions are based.

- **LEVEL 1: Remember**
  Define stress.
- **LEVEL 2: Understand**
  Explain the difference between eustress and distress.
- **LEVEL 3: Apply**
  Apply three actions you can take to relieve your personal stress.
- **LEVEL 4: Analyze**
  Compare and contrast situational, psychological, and biological stress.
- **LEVEL 5: Evaluate**
  Recommend strategies to a friend who is dealing with extreme pressures.
- **LEVEL 6: Create**
  Design a stress management plan that addresses most of your personal stressors.

MyStudentSuccessLab

MyStudentSuccessLab is an online solution designed to help you acquire and develop (or hone) the skills you need to succeed. You will have access to peer-led video presentations and develop core skills through interactive exercises and projects.

STRESS? I DON'T HAVE ENOUGH TIME FOR STRESS!

Do You Feel Like You're Going to Explode?

The word *stress* is derived from the Latin word **strictus,** meaning "to draw tight." Stress is your body's response to people and events in your life; it is the mental and physical wear and tear on your body as a result of everyday life and all that you have to accomplish. Stress is inevitable, and it is not in itself bad. It is your response to stress that determines whether it is good stress (**eustress**) or bad stress (**distress**) or **positive** and **negative stress.** Positive stress improves productivity provided it doesn't persist too long. Negative stress, on the other hand, can impact you both physically and mentally.

Some physical signs of distress (bad stress) are:

"*The right amount of stress can actually be helpful. The idea is that pressure pushes people to improve themselves and take new risks.*"

—Nicole Keeter

Headaches	Muscular tension and pain	Fatigue
Coughs	Abdominal pain and diarrhea	Mental disorders
Dry mouth	Hypertension and chest pain	Insomnia
Impotence	Heartburn and indigestion	Suicidal tendencies
Twitching/trembling	Abdominal pain	Apprehension
Jitters	Diminished performance	Decreased coping ability

If you begin to experience any of these reactions for an extended period of time, you know that your body and mind are probably suffering from undue stress, anxiety, and pressure. This can lead to a very unhealthy situation. Take the "Stress Test" in Figure 11.1 to determine your level of stress.

Figure 11.1 Test Your Stress

Take the following **Stress Assessment** to determine the level of distress you are currently experiencing in your life—check the items that reflect your behavior at home, work, or school, or in a social setting.

❑ 1. Your stomach tightens when you think about your work and all that you have to do.

❑ 2. You are not able to sleep at night.

❑ 3. You race from place to place trying to get everything done that is required of you.

❑ 4. Small things make you angry.

(continued)

❑ 5. At the end of the day, you are frustrated that you did not accomplish all that you needed to do.

❑ 6. You get tired throughout the day.

❑ 7. You need some type of drug, alcohol, or tobacco to get through the day.

❑ 8. You often find it hard to be around people.

❑ 9. You don't take care of yourself physically or mentally.

❑ 10. You tend to keep everything inside.

❑ 11. You overreact.

❑ 12. You fail to find the humor in many situations others see as funny.

❑ 13. You do not eat properly.

❑ 14. Everything upsets you.

❑ 15. You are impatient and get angry when you have to wait for things.

❑ 16. You don't trust others.

❑ 17. You feel that most people move too slowly for you.

❑ 18. You feel guilty when you take time for yourself or your friends.

❑ 19. You interrupt people so that you can tell them your side of the story.

❑ 20. You experience memory loss.

Total Number of Check Marks = _____

0–5 = Low, manageable stress

6–10 = Moderate stress

11+ = High stress, could cause medical or emotional problems

MAJOR STRESSORS THAT AFFECT STUDENTS

How Can Controlling the Demons of Stress Help?

For many people, college can be a stressful time. Many students have to pay their tuition, rent, food bills, car payments, insurance, and childcare, and they have that nagging feeling about student loans that is always with them. Oh, and there are instructors who seem to think students have nothing else to do but write another paper and study for another test. So, let's come to grips with some of the major stressors and what you can do about them. Study the following and try to identify which stressors apply to you.

1. **Money pressures.** Many students have to pay their own way through school these days with very little assistance. Knowing you have to pay tuition, buy books, provide for your housing, and, perhaps, also provide for family and others creates monumental stress. Students who have scholarships feel great pressure to earn high grades so they don't lose their assistance.

2. **Time management and organization skills.** Students are just plain busy, and you have so much to get done—many have to work; others are officers in clubs or play sports; some have to meet community service project responsibilities. Many have families.

3. **Tests, grades, and projects.** Tests, projects, papers, and grades are constantly gnawing at students and put intense pressure on you to perform. So much is riding on grades, and this brings intense stress for many. Academic competition has never been more fierce, with GPAs and SAT and ACT scores higher than ever before. Some parents, who are stressed themselves if they are trying to help pay for school, may put inordinate amounts of pressure on you to perform well so you can graduate and get a good job.

4. **Sleep deprivation.** We are all grouchy and disoriented when we lose too much sleep, and this is a common problem for students. You may work too many hours trying to keep your head above water; stay out too late; or wait until the last minute to study for a test and stay up all night cramming. Many students suffer from sleep deprivation, much of it brought on by failing to take responsibility to do the right things at the right time.

How do your relationships affect your stress levels?
Fotolia

5. **Relationships.** Classmates, roommates, boyfriends, girlfriends, partners, friends—all can cause stress for students. Students may be thrown together with roommates with whom they have nothing in common. You may feel stress in trying to find the right person, then the stress of having to spend time with that person once you find Mr. or Miss Right. Some students have long-distance relationships, and they spend lots of time worrying about their significant other's faithfulness.

TIPS FOR RELIEVING STRESS

What Is the Relationship between Stress and Your Health?

There are probably as many stressors in this world as there are people alive. One thing is for sure: poor planning and "running out of time" are on most people's list of major stressors. There is no doubt that effective priority management and stress management go hand in hand.

Because of poor planning and procrastination, we become anxious and nervous about not getting it all done. By planning, prioritizing, and developing a strategy, we can actually lower our stress level and improve our general, overall health and our memory. Medical research has shown that exposure to stress over a long period of time can be damaging to your health.

Physical symptoms include ***exhaustion***, where one part of the body weakens and shifts its responsibility to another part and causes complete failure of key organ functions. ***Chronic muscle pain*** and malfunction are also affected by unchecked stress. "Chronically tense muscles also result in numerous stress-related disorders including headaches, backaches, spasms of the esophagus and colon (causing diarrhea and constipation), posture problems, asthma, tightness in the throat and chest cavity, some eye problems, lockjaw, muscle tears and pulls, and perhaps rheumatoid arthritis" (Girdano, Dusek, & Everly, 2009).

As you can see, stress is not something that you can just ignore and hope it will go away. Study the tips for relieving stress in Figure 11.2.

Figure 11.2   Tips for Relieving Stress

- Become a dedicated goal setter and list maker and follow your plans carefully. One of the greatest causes of stress is floundering, not knowing where you are going.

- Reduce your intake of alcohol, which can cause your moods to fluctuate and can make you edgy.

- Avoid using any drugs because they will cost you in every way possible—health, grades, relationships, financial, job. If you smoke, quit! In addition to being damaging to your health, nicotine is a stimulant and overstresses your body.

- Eat well. Certain foods give your body energy, while others drain your vitality. Reduce sweets and carbohydrates and increase proteins such as lean meats and fish. Put more fruits and vegetables in your diet. Reduce your caffeine intake.

- Exercise! Physical exercise actually takes stress out of your body. If you feel yourself getting uptight, stop what you are doing and take a brisk 15-minute walk.

- End unhealthy relationships—friends, boyfriends, girlfriends, and, yes, maybe even some family members. Toxic people stress us out!

- Get rid of all the clutter in your life because things have to be cared for. Sometimes we can become "possessed by our possessions." Simplify your life!

- Understand your peak times and schedule your most important activities during those times if possible.

- Turn off your computer and smartphone for at least one hour per day. Devote this time to planning, studying, thinking, and just being quiet.

- Use relaxation techniques, such as visualization, listening to music, and practicing yoga.

- Get enough rest. You may not need eight hours, but your body needs a certain amount of sleep to regenerate itself.

- Spend time with pets because it lowers your heart rate.

- Take a hot bath or a long, hot shower.

- Laugh often! Laughter has been shown to increase learning and retention by 800 percent!

- Plan both long- and short-joy breaks. Go for a walk with a friend. Go home for the weekend if you live away. Watch a good movie. Read a good book.

- Put "sacred days" on your calendar and let nothing supplant them. Make them special events in your life to look forward to that will reward you for sticking to your schedule.

- Strive for balance in all aspects of your life—emotionally, physically, mentally, and spiritually.

Examine Figure 11.3 to understand major stressors in your life. Thinking creatively, decide on three new and unusual "joy breaks" that would help you relieve your stress. List them in the space below and write a deadline beside each one. Write three "sacred day" events that you could look forward to. Put the date beside each event.

Figure 11.3   Taking a Joy Break

JOY BREAKS	DEADLINE	SACRED DAYS	DATE

Most of the things that cause us stress fall into one of three categories:

■ **Situational stress** is related to your surroundings, how you use time management, if you say "yes" when you should have said "no."

■ **Psychological stress** is a feeling that one cannot cope with a particular challenge.

■ **Biological stress** is caused by stressors that impact your body's functions, such as not being able to sleep.

Study the three types of major stressors in Figure 11.4 and identify those that cause you the most stress.

Figure 11.4   Three Types of Major Stressors in Life

TYPE	CAUSE	WHAT YOU CAN DO TO REDUCE STRESS
Situational	Change in physical environment	■ If at all possible, change your residence or physical environment to better suit your needs. ■ If you can't change it, talk to the people involved and explain your feelings.
	Change in social environment	■ Work hard to meet new friends who support you and upon whom you can rely in times of need. ■ Get involved in some type of activity outside of work. ■ Join a group activity or sport team.
	Daily hassles	■ Try to keep things in perspective and work to reduce the things that you allow to stress you out. ■ Allow time in your schedule for unexpected events. ■ Find a quiet place to relax and think.
	Poor time management	■ Work out a time management plan that allows time to get your work completed while allowing time for rest and joy, too. ■ Create "to-do" lists.
	Conflicts at work and home	■ Read about conflict management and realize that conflict can result in stress. ■ Avoid "hot" topics such as religion or politics if you feel this causes you to engage in conflicts. ■ Be assertive, not aggressive or rude.
	People	■ Try to avoid people who stress you out. ■ Put people into perspective and realize that we're all different with different needs, wants, and desires. ■ Realize that everyone is not going to be like you and everyone is not going to like you.
	Relationships	■ Work hard to develop healthy, positive relationships. ■ Move away from toxic, unhealthy relationships and people who bring you down. ■ Understand that you can *never* change the way another person feels, acts, or thinks.
	Death of a loved one	■ Try to focus on the good times you shared and what they meant to your life. ■ Remember that death is as much a part of life as living. ■ Talk about the person with your friends and family—share your memories. ■ Consider what the deceased person would have wanted you to do.

(continued)

TYPE	CAUSE	WHAT YOU CAN DO TO REDUCE STRESS
	Financial problems	■ Cut back on your spending. ■ Seek the help of a financial planner. ■ Determine why your financial planning or spending patterns are causing you problems.
Psychological	Unrealistic expectations	■ Surround yourself with positive people and work hard to set realistic goals with doable timelines and results. ■ Expect and anticipate less.
	Loneliness	■ Surround yourself with people who support you. ■ Call or visit home as often as you can until you get more comfortable. ■ Meet new friends at work or in your neighborhood.
	Fear	■ Plan and execute carefully to help you feel more confident. ■ Visualize success and not failure. ■ Do one thing every day that scares you to expand your comfort zone.
	Anxiety over your future and what is going to happen	■ Put things into perspective and work hard to plan and prepare, but accept that life is about constant change. ■ Don't try to control the uncontrollable. ■ Try to see the big picture and how "the puzzle" is going to come together.
	Anxiety over your past	■ Work hard to overcome past challenges and remember that your past does not have to dictate your future. ■ Learn to forgive. ■ Focus on your future and what you really want to accomplish.
Biological	Insomnia	■ Watch your caffeine intake. ■ Avoid naps. ■ Do not exercise two hours prior to your normal bedtime. ■ Complete all of your activities before going to bed (working, watching TV, e-mailing, texting, etc.)—your bed is for sleeping.
	Anxiety	■ Laugh more. Share a joke. ■ Enjoy your friends and family. ■ Practice breathing exercises. ■ Talk it out with friends. ■ Learn to say "No" and mean it. ■ Turn off the TV if the news makes you anxious or nervous.
	Weight loss/gain	■ Develop an exercise and healthy eating plan. ■ Meet with a nutrition specialist. ■ Join a health-related club or gym.
	Reduced physical activities	■ Increase your daily activity. ■ If possible, walk to work or lunch instead of driving. ■ Take the stairs instead of the elevator.
	Sexual difficulties/ dysfunction	■ Seek medical help in case something is physically wrong. ■ Determine if your actions are in contradiction with your value system.

from ordinary to

Extraordinary

Maureen Riopelle, President & Founder, Mary's Circle of Hope — The Mary Maguire Foundation, Milford, OH

Things could not have been going better! Maureen was a star basketball player recruited by hundreds of colleges and was a top pick by the University of Iowa. Her dream of going to college, becoming an Olympic athlete, and later a sportscaster was so close she could see it all happening. But, life has a funny way of turning on a dime.

Maureen had suffered knee problems for many years. Most doctors attributed it to "growing pains." She continued to play sports in high school despite the pain. When she got to the University of Iowa, at the urging of her coaches, she finally saw a few specialists who reported that she had lost 35 percent of her capacity and recommended surgery. After the surgery, her knees actually began to worsen, and additional surgery was scheduled. Maureen was told that she would probably have to have surgery every two years to repair the damage to her knees and that she only had a 50/50 chance of ever walking again.

She had five surgeries in seven months, but within a year she was walking, and within a year and a half, she walked her first 5K. She went back to college and graduated with a 4.0 GPA and began her career, only to face another devastating illness.

She was diagnosed with breast cancer that had spread to her lymph nodes. Her determination and strong will to live and beat the odds became her salvation once again.

After surgery and treatment, there are no signs of cancer. Because of these challenging experiences, Maureen found her life's calling. She founded *Mary's Circle of Hope—The Mary Maguire Foundation*, a non-profit organization dedicated to the support of women cancer survivors. She moved from ordinary to extraordinary!

> *Maureen was told that she would probably have to have surgery every two years to repair the damage to her knees and that she only had a 50/50 chance of ever walking again.*

EXTRAORDINARY REFLECTION

Ms. Riopelle suffered several major setbacks with her health problems, yet she overcame these problems and turned her life into a positive force to help others. What advice would you give to someone who is facing a major life-threatening health problem with regard to persistence, internal motivation, positive thinking, and determination?

REFLECTIONS
Dealing Positively with Stress

Learning to deal with stress in a positive manner is a skill that you will need for the rest of your life. By learning to avoid procrastination and taking the time to enhance the quality of your life through reduced stress, you will live a more fulfilled and enjoyable life. Simplify your life, take time to smell the roses, and manage your time so you can have more fun! Organize your time, stick to a schedule, find a good place to study, and work before you play. Use technology in ways to reduce your stress rather than enhancing it. Stress can be positive if used properly and if you don't overdose on it.

Knowledge in Bloom

CREATING A STRESS MANAGEMENT PLAN

Each lesson-end assessment is based on Bloom's Taxonomy of Learning. See the first page of this lesson for a quick review.

This activity uses levels 4–6 of the taxonomy

Using the example below, complete the following stress management plan. Think about things that cause you stress and determine ways to deal with them. Study the examples that are provided to help you get started. Stressors in the following example are calculus, procrastination, and a relationship. A description of each stressor is placed under the type of stressor. Finally, an action plan to deal with the stressor is included in the last column. You may have to conduct research to find the solutions to some of your stressors.

MY PERSONAL STRESS MANAGEMENT PLAN

Certain things, people, events, courses, and so forth stress me out the most. When I am stressed, I exhibit certain symptoms, feelings, and negative behaviors. Some of my stressors are physical, emotional, mental, and spiritual. My plan is to learn how to reduce each type of stress.

Stressor	Physical	Emotional	Mental	Spiritual	Action
Calculus			I get very uptight when I have a test.		I will form a study group and get a tutor.
Procrastination	I get physically ill when deadlines approach because I have not used my time wisely.				I will make a schedule for all my courses, assignments, and work daily to stay on track.
Relationship		I want to break up with Bob but he has a violent temper, and I don't know what to do.			I will seek counseling and report his behavior to the proper authorities.

Using this example, **design your own stress management plan** using major stressors in your life.

Stressor	Physical	Emotional	Mental	Spiritual	Action

REFERENCE

Girdano, D., Dusek, D., & Everly, G. (2009). *Controlling Stress and Tension* (8th ed.). Boston, MA: Benjamin Cummings.

PLAN

CREATING A DYNAMIC EMPLOYMENT PACKAGE AND JOB SEARCH PLAN

Shutterstock

"We cannot become what we are capable of being by remaining who we are." —Unknown

PLAN

PLAN

Why read this lesson?

Because you'll learn how to:

- Create a career exploration plan

Because you'll be able to:

- Describe careers related to your interests
- Explain the key strategies for exploring a career
- Recommend strategies for networking that enhance career exploration and growth
- Create a resume

Knowledge in Bloom

Bloom's Taxonomy of Learning is a simple way of explaining the levels at which we all learn material and acquire information. The learning levels progress from basic to more complex learning and thinking. Examples are detailed below. Throughout this lesson, you'll see colorful triangles to the side of some activities. They let you know on which level of Bloom's Taxonomy the questions are based.

- **LEVEL 1: Remember**
  List five things you should consider when deciding on a career.
- **LEVEL 2: Understand**
  Explain how your personality type affects your career choice
- **LEVEL 3: Apply**
  Demonstrate appropriate dress for an interview.
- **LEVEL 4: Analyze**
  Distinguish between a career and a job.
- **LEVEL 5: Evaluate**
  Recommend strategies for seeking help relative to your career search.
- **LEVEL 6: Create**
  Compose a cover letter and resume.

MyStudentSuccessLab

MyStudentSuccessLab is an online solution designed to help you acquire and develop (or hone) the skills you need to succeed. You will have access to peer-led video presentations and develop core skills through interactive exercises and projects.

EXPLORING CAREER OPTIONS

What Am I Going to Do for the Rest of My Life?

"What am I going to do for the rest of my life?" is an overwhelming question. You have a wonderful opportunity to function in a world economy; at the same time, you may be challenged by having fewer guidelines to follow.

It is likely that you will have many different jobs during your lifetime—including three to four different careers—and what constitutes your work will be constantly changing. Because the workplace has changed so much, it has become increasingly important for college students to begin thinking about career options early and often.

First, Know Yourself

Answer the following questions that will help guide you in your personal career exploration.

What are your major interests? _____

_____

How can these interests be transferred to a career choice? _____

_____

_____

Level 5 Evaluate

Do You Enjoy Physical or Mental Work?

Many people would go crazy if they had to spend as much as one hour per day in an office. Others would be unhappy if they had to work in the sun all day.

Do you enjoy physical or mental work or both? Why? _____

_____

What does this mean to your career path? _____

_____

_____

What Is Most Important? Money? Service? Independence? Or a Combination?

Most people, if asked, "Why do you work?" would respond, "For the money." There is nothing wrong with wanting to make money in your profession, but not all professions, regardless of their worth, pay well. Some of the hardest and most rewarding work pays the least.

Is your major goal in choosing a profession, money or something else? What? _____

_____

What does your goal mean to your career path? _____

_____

_____

Where Do You Want to Live?

Although this question may sound strange, many careers are limited by geography. Some people simply prefer certain parts of the country (or the world) to others.

Where do you eventually want to live? Why? _____

_____

What does your preference mean to your career path? _____

_____

_____

Do You Want to Travel?

Some jobs require travel; some people love to travel, some hate it. Ask yourself whether you want to be away from your home and family four nights per week, or whether you want a job that does not require any travel.

Do you enjoy travel? Do you want to do a lot of traveling? _____

_____

What does this mean to your career path? _____

_____

_____

What Motivates You?

What are the one or two things in your life that motivate you? Money? Power? Helping other people? The answer to this question is an essential element to choosing a career.

What is your motivational force and why? _____

_____

How could this help you in deciding on a career path? _____

_____

_____

What Do You Value?

Do you value relationships, possessions, money, love, security, challenges, or power? Once you have identified what you value in your life, you can identify careers that closely match your personal value system and eliminate careers that don't.

What do you truly value in your life? _____

_____

How might these values affect your career decisions? _____

_____

_____

What Are Your Skills?

Are you especially good at one or two things? Are you good with computers, a good manager of money, a good carpenter, a good communicator? Your skills will play a powerful part in selecting a career. Employers still stress the importance of three basic skills: writing, speaking, and listening. If you have these skills, you are ahead of the pack.

What are your skills? What do you do well? _____

_____

How could your strongest skills help you make a career decision? _____

_____

_____

Are You a Leader?

One of the most important questions you must ask yourself is, "Do I enjoy leading, teaching, or guiding people?" If you prefer to be part of the crowd and do not like to stand out as a leader or manager, some careers may not suit you. If you like to take charge and get things done when you are with other people, you will find certain careers better than others.

Do you consider yourself a leader? _____

_____

How do you feel about managing other people? _____

_____

_____

STRATEGIES FOR CAREER EXPLORATION

Where Do I Search for Career Options?

If you have no idea what you want to do when you graduate or if you are still undecided about the focus of your career after graduation, you are not all that unusual. You don't have to decide today, but you do need to begin exploring career options. Consider the following **Tips for Career Exploration.** They can help you refine choices.

1. **Dream!** If money were not a problem or concern, what would you do for the rest of your life? If you could do anything in the world, what would you do? Where would you do it?

Can you learn to anticipate "where the puck is going" as it relates to your future?
UK History/Alamy

These are the types of questions you must ask yourself as you select a major and a career.

2. **Go where the puck is going!** Sound crazy? The great hockey champ Wayne Gretzky made the comment that *this one step* had been his key to success. What does it mean? He said that when he was playing hockey, he did not skate to where the puck was at the moment, he skated to where the puck was *going*. He anticipated the direction of where it was going to be hit, and when it came his way, he was already there—ready to play. Think of your career in this light. Go to where the future is bright, not necessarily where it is bright at this moment.

3. **Talk to your advisor.** Academic advisors are there to help you. But don't be surprised if their doors are sometimes closed. They teach, conduct research, perform community service, and sometimes advise hundreds of students. Always call in advance and make an appointment to see an advisor. When you have that appointment, make your advisor work for you. Take your college catalog and ask questions, hard questions.

4. **Use electives.** The accreditation agency that works with your school requires that you be allowed at least one free elective in your degree program. Some programs allow many more. Use your electives wisely! Do not take courses just to get the hours. The wisest students use their electives to delve into new areas of interest or to take a block of courses in an area that might enhance their career opportunities.

5. **Go to your school's career center.** Most schools' career centers provide free services. The same types of services in the community could cost from $200 to $2,000. The professionals in the career center can provide information on a variety of careers and fields, and they can administer interest and personality inventories that can help you decide your major and narrow your career choices.

6. **Read, read, read!** Nothing will help you more than reading about careers and majors. Ask your advisor or counselor to help you locate information on your areas of interest. Gather information from colleges, agencies, associations, and places of employment. Then read it!

7. **Job Shadow.** Shadowing describes the process of following someone around on the job. If you are wondering what engineers, for example, do on the job, try calling an engineering office to see whether you can sit with several of their engineers for a day over spring break.

8. **Join pre-professional organizations.** One of the most important steps you can take as a college student is to become involved in campus organizations and clubs that offer educational opportunities, social interaction, and hands-on experience in your chosen field. Pre-professional organizations can open doors that will help you make a career decision.

9. **Get a part-time job.** Work in an area that you may be interested in pursuing as a career. Get a part-time job while you are in school or work in a related job in the summer.

10. **Try to get a summer practicum or internship.** Work in your field of interest to gain practical experience and see if it really suits you. Some programs require a practicum or internship, and this experience often leads to your first full-time job.

By working through this ten-step plan, you will come closer to finding what you really want and need in your life's work. Take your time, study, read, ask questions, shadow others, and most importantly, make your own decision. Yes, you may change majors or even careers along the way, but that is a part of life's journey.

Your Dream Job

Using the answers you provided to the previous questions and additional resources, such as academic or career advisors, write a description for your dream job—the job you would have if you could do anything you would like to do.

Level 3 Apply

_____

_____

_____

BUILDING A BUSINESS NETWORK FOR THE FUTURE

Is It Really Who You Know?

You've all heard the expression, "It's not what you know, but who you know." Well, few statements could be more true, and college is the perfect place for making many personal and professional contacts. At this moment, you are building a network of people on whom you can call for the rest of your life.

Networking is one of the most important aspects of career development. Who do you know or who would you like to get to know who could be valued members of your personal network? You might consider the following types of people:

- **Cornerstones.** These people form the foundation of your network. They might include instructors, people for whom you have worked, friends of your family, parents of your friends—people you know you can rely on.
- **Experts in your field of interest.** Once you decide on the career you want to pursue, you can seek an expert whom you might shadow; you might shadow several. These people may become valuable members of your network.
- **Role models.** This might be someone at your college or workplace whom you look up to and admire. Ask the person questions, and let him or her know you value their advice.
- **Mentors.** Mentors can be very valuable to you because they take a special interest in you and your future. Mentors can open doors for you and help you in your professional development as you move through your career.

UNDERSTANDING THE DO'S AND DON'TS OF A POWERFUL JOB SEARCH PLAN

What Does It Take To Get A Foot In the Door?

The most important part of the job search process is the preparation that must be done **_prior to starting_** the interview process. A carefully crafted cover letter and resume communicate your past history (education, skills, and experience) that makes you the ideal candidate for a position. They are the first marketing pieces a recruiter sees when determining whether or not to interview you.

Figure 12.1　General Tips for the Cover Letter and Resume

- Both your resume and cover letter *must be typed*. There are no exceptions to this rule. Ever! Seriously, EVER!

- Your cover letter and resume must be printed on the same *type and color* of *fine-quality paper*. Cheap paper sends the message that you don't care. This is not the place or time to pinch pennies; buy excellent quality, 100% cotton stock, resume-quality paper.

- Check your printer and be sure that the print quality is impeccable. Never send a cover letter or resume with smudges, ink smears, or poor print quality.

- When you print your cover letter and resume, be certain that the watermark on the paper is turned in the correct direction. Hold it up to the light and you will see the watermark embedded in the paper. This may sound silly and picky, but people notice attention to detail.

- Do not fold your cover letter or resume. Purchase a packet of 9 × 13 envelopes in which to send your materials.

- Do not handwrite the address on the envelope. Use a label or type the address directly on the envelope. Remember, first impressions are important.

- Never send a generic photocopy of a cover letter or resume, even on the finest paper.

- Layout, design, font, spacing, and color must be considered in the building of your cover letter and resume.

- Unless you are specifically asked to do so, never discuss money or salary history in either your cover letter or resume. This could work against you. When asked for a salary history, use ranges.

- Your resume and cover letter must be error-free. That's right, not one single error is acceptable including grammar, spelling, punctuation, layout/spacing, dates, or content.

- Each cover letter must be signed in black or blue ink.

Writing a Powerful Cover Letter and Resume

As you begin writing cover letters and resumes, a good thing to remember is this: A resume and cover letter get you the interview; the interview gets you the job.

A **cover letter** is basically an expansion of your resume. A cover letter gives you the chance to link your resume, skills, and experience together with your interest in a specific company's position and their advertising. You will need to write many cover letters to make this link work properly; in other words, you most likely need to write a cover letter designed for each job for which you apply. One generic cover letter is not acceptable. Your cover letter will often be the stepping stone to get an employer to even look at your resume. Examine Figure 12.1 to determine the components of an effective cover letter and Figure 12.2 to see an example of an actual cover letter.

UNDERSTAND THE DO'S AND DON'TS OF MEMORABLE RESUMES

How Do You Sell Yourself?

A resume is the blueprint that details what you have accomplished with regard to education, experience, skills acquisition, workplace successes, and progressive responsibility and/or leadership. It is the ultimate advertisement of *you*!

Figure 12.2 Sample Cover Letter with Formatting Information

Your name and address ———▶	**BENJAMIN SHAW**
Your name should be larger and/or in a different font to draw attention (then double space)	1234 Lake Shadow Drive (123) 555-1234 Maple City, PA 12345 Benjamin@bl.com
The date (then double space) ———▶	January 3, 2011
The specific person, title, and address to whom you are writing (then double space) ———▶	Mr. James Pixler, RN, CAN Director of Placement and Advancement Grace Care Center 123 Sizemore Street, Suite 444 Philadelphia, PA 12345
The formal salutation followed by a colon (then double space) ———▶	Dear Mr. Pixler:
Paragraph 1 (then double space) ———▶	Seven years ago, my mother was under the treatment of two incredible nurses at Grace Care Center in Philadelphia. My family and I agree that the care she was given was extraordinary. When I saw your ad in today's Philadelphia Carrier, I was extremely pleased to know that I now have the qualifications to be a part of the Grace Care Team as a Medical Assistant.
Paragraph 2 (then double space) ———▶	Next month, I will graduate with an Occupational Associate's Degree from Victory College of Health and Technology as a certified Medical Assistant. As my resume indicates, I was fortunate to do my internship at Mercy Family Care Practice in Harrisburg. During this time, I was directly involved in patient care, records documentation, and family outreach.
Paragraph 3 (then double space) ———▶	As a part of my degree from Victory, I received a 4.0 in the following classes: • Management Communications • Microsoft Office (Word, Excel, Outlook, PowerPoint) • Business Communications I, II, III • Anatomy and Physiology I, II, III • Medical Coding I, II • Principles of Pharmacology • Immunology I, II, III, IV • Urinalysis and Body Fluids • Clinical Practicum I, II, III This, along with my past certificate in Medical Transcription and my immense respect for Grace Care Center, makes me the perfect candidate for your position.
Final paragraph or closing (then double space) ———▶	I have detailed all of my experience on the enclosed resume. I will call you on Monday, January 24, at 11:30 a.m. to discuss how my education and experiences can help streamline operations and continue superior patient care at Grace. In the meantime, please feel free to contact me at the number above.
The complimentary close and comma (then four spaces) ———▶	Sincerely,
Your handwritten signature in black or blue ink within the four spaces ———▶	*Benjamin Shaw*
Your typed name ———▶	Benjamin Shaw
Enclosure contents ———▶	Enclosure: Resume

Further, your resume must be 100% completely accurate and truthful. Do not fabricate information or fudge dates to make yourself look better. It will only come back to haunt you in the long run. Dennis Reina, organizational psychologist and author of *Trust and Betrayal in the Workplace,* states, "I think that what you put in a resume absolutely has to be rock-solid, concrete, and verifiable. If there are any questions, it will immediately throw both your application and your credibility into question" (Dresang, 2007).

As you begin to build your resume, remember to "call in the **D.O.C.T.O.R.**"

D: Design

Visual **design** and format are imperative to a successful resume. You need to think about the font that you plan to use, whether color is appropriate (usually, it is not), the use of bullets, lines, or shading, and where you are going to put information. You also need to pay attention to the text balance on the page (centered left/right, top/bottom). The visual aspect of your resume will be the first impression. "Make it pretty" (Britton-Whitcomb, 2003).

O: Objective

Writing a clear and specific **objective** can help get your foot in the door. The reader, usually your potential employer, needs to be able to scan your resume and gather as much detail as possible as quickly as possible. A job-specific objective can help. Consider the following objective:

> **Objective:** To secure an elementary teaching position that will enable me to use my 14 years of creative teaching experience, curriculum development abilities, supervisory skills, and commitment to superior instruction in a team environment.

C: Clarity

Clarity is of paramount importance, especially when including your past responsibilities, education, and job responsibilities. Be certain that you let the reader know exactly what you have done, what specific education you have gained, and what progress you have made. Being vague and unclear can cost you an interview.

T: Truth

When writing your resume, you may be tempted to fudge a little bit here and there to make your resume look better. Perhaps you were out of work for a few months and you think it looks bad to have this gap in your chronological history. Avoid the urge to fudge. Telling the absolute **truth** on a resume is essential.

O: Organization

Before you begin your resume, think about the **organization** of your data. You will be provided a model resume in this chapter; however, there are several other formats you might select.

R: Review

Reviewing your resume and cover letter is important, but having someone else review them for clarity, accuracy, spelling, grammar, placement, and overall content can be one of the best things you can do for your job search. In Figure 12.3, you will see a sample resume. Study this example as you begin to build your resume and career search package.

Figure 12.3 **Sample Resume**

BENJAMIN SHAW

1234 Lake Shadow Drive, Maple City, p. 12345   (123) 555-1234   Benjamin@bl.com

OBJECTIVE: To work as a medical assistant in an atmosphere that uses my organizational skills, compassion for people, desire to make a difference, and impeccable work ethic.

PROFESSIONAL EXPERIENCE:

January 2007–Present

Medical Assistant Intern

Mercy Family Care Practice, Harrisburg, PA
- Responsible for completing patient charts
- Take patients' vitals
- Assist with medical coding

February 2003–December 2006

Medical Transcriptionist
The Office of Brenda Wilson, MD, Lancaster, PA
- Interpreted and typed medical reports
- Worked with insurance documentation
- Assisted with medical coding
- Served as Office Manager (1/05–12/06)

March 1998–February 2003

Ward Orderly
Wallace Hospital, Lancaster, PA
- Assisted nurses with patient care
- Cleaned patient rooms
- Served patient meals

August 1995–March 1998

Administrative Assistant
Ellen Abbot Nursing Care Facility
- Typed office reports
- Organized patient files

EDUCATION:

Occupational Associate's Degree—Medical Assistant
Victory Health Institute, Harrisburg, PA
May 2008 (with honors)

Certificate of Completion—Medical Transcription
Philadelphia Technical Institute
December 2002

Vocational High School Diploma—Health Sciences
Philadelphia Vocational High School
August 1995

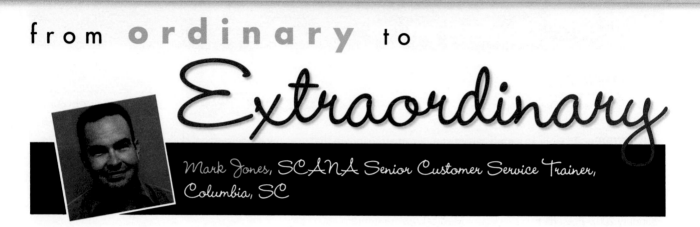

from **ordinary** to

Extraordinary

Mark Jones, SCANA Senior Customer Service Trainer, Columbia, SC

Mark Jones likes to refer to himself as a functional member of a dysfunctional family. His mother was clinically depressed all Mark's life and was always heavily medicated. She attempted suicide when he was just four years old. His father had the first of four heart attacks when Mark was only six. When he was 11, his parents divorced, and he went to live with his father. His mother remarried when he was 13. His father died when he was 15, leaving his family very little in the way of financial support. Even the mobile home in which they lived was repossessed. His new stepfather was legally blind and his mother did not drive either. Consequently, they didn't want Mark to drive. His stepfather treated **Mark** like a tenant, requiring him to pay rent from the small Social Security check he drew from his father's account. He even had to buy his own bed. Mark knew this situation was far from "normal," and he was determined to escape and live a better life. One of his proudest moments was realizing, "I don't have to be like them."

When he was in his early twenties, he bought a car for $200, and even though the old Buick LeSabre had been used

> *When he was in his early twenties, he bought a car for $200, and even though the old Buick LeSabre had been used in demolition donut field races and had been wrecked down one side, it gave him freedom.*

in demolition donut field races and had been wrecked down one side, it gave him freedom. He enrolled in college but soon had to drop out because he couldn't afford tuition. He knew he didn't want to live the life of his parents, so he began searching for a job with a company that had educational benefits. He learned to craft his resume to meet a company's needs, and he finally got a job with educational benefits, and was able to buy a better car.

Mark worked his way up in the big utilities company where he first went to work, and today he is a Senior Customer Service Trainer. Mark did not let his past or his troubled family dictate his future. He moved from ordinary to extraordinary!

EXTRAORDINARY REFLECTION

Mr. Jones came from a family that did not support him financially, emotionally, or educationally. What advice would you give to someone who might be experiencing the same type of environment? In your opinion, does your family have to play a role in your life for you to be successful?

PREPARING FOR THE INTERVIEW

What's All the Fuss About?

As you prepare for your interview, consider the following sound advice:

DAYS BEFORE THE INTERVIEW

- Prepare extra copies of your resume to take to the interview. Though one person typically conducts interviews, some employers designate several people to sit in on the interview process.

- Place your extra resumes, references, and other job search information in a professional portfolio (leather binder) or nice folder.
- Prepare a typed reference sheet and take several copies to the interview.
- If achievement portfolios are required, update your portfolio with any last-minute, applicable information.
- Using the research that you have done on the company, make a list of questions that you want to ask the interviewer. Never attend an interview without asking questions yourself.
- Ask someone whose opinion you trust to look at your interview outfit and give you advice and suggestions for improvement.

THE DAY OF, AND ON THE WAY TO, THE INTERVIEW

- Get up early and spend some time alone reviewing the job announcement, your resume, your portfolio, the company's profile, and other important information.
- Bring a pen, paper, and calendar with you to the interview. These can be kept in your portfolio, too.
- Be certain that your clothes are clean and pressed, and your shoes are shined.
- Arrive at the interview at least 15 minutes early.
- If you are a smoker, **do not** smoke in the car on the way to the interview and try to avoid smoking in your interview clothes.
- Before you enter the building, **turn off** your cell phone, pager, Blackberry, iPod, and any other electronic devices. **Turn them off**. Period!

DURING THE INTERVIEW

- Establish eye contact. When you enter, shake hands firmly with everyone in the room.
- Speak with clarity and enunciate your words. Enter with a positive and upbeat attitude.
- Ask where to sit if you are not told upon entering the room.
- Jot down the names of everyone in the room as they are introduced to you.
- Refer to people by their names if you address them during the interview.
- You don't have to be deadly serious or stodgy, but it is advisable to avoid jokes or off-color humor, as well as political leanings and religious beliefs.
- Consider your grammar and strive to use correct speech.
- **Never** downgrade or talk badly about a past job or employer. This will only come back to haunt you.
- If you are offered anything to eat or drink, accept only water just in case your mouth becomes dry during the interview.
- **Never** ask about money or company benefits during an interview, especially during the *first* interview, unless the interviewer approaches the topic.

AFTER THE INTERVIEW

- Shake hands with everyone in the room and thank them for the opportunity to meet with them. Let them know that you were honored to have the opportunity and that you are very interested in the position.
- Ask each person in the room for a business card. This provides you their correct name spelling, address, and e-mail address.
- Always follow up with a personalized thank you note.

REFLECTIONS on Career Management

College is a growing time for you and you might discover new interests and directions that you have never considered before. Follow your heart, and pursue your dreams. If there is something you have always wanted to do or be, chances are your desires will not change even after you study other options.

This is your one lifetime! You need to prepare to do something you love. No matter how much money you make, you won't be happy unless you are doing something that matters to you, something that allows you to keep learning and growing, and something that provides you with opportunities to give back.

Knowledge in Bloom

CONNECTING ON LINKEDIN

Each lesson-end assessment is based on Bloom's Taxonomy of Learning. See the first page of this lesson for a quick review.

This activity uses levels 3 and 6 of the taxonomy

One of the most widely used and popular social media sites for employees and employers today is LinkedIn. This site is career oriented and connects people who are looking for jobs with those who are searching for employees. LinkedIn allows you to post your resume and recommendations from your references; you can connect with former bosses and colleagues; and you can form groups who might like to discuss similar topics. Since your LinkedIn profile is very much like an online interactive resume, you need to take special care when you set up your account. Go to www.linkedin.com and click on "Join Today." Once you have set up your account and read the User Agreement and Privacy Policy, you should write your summary statement. Use action words to sell your accomplishments; use keywords that make it easy for industry people to locate you. Treat your summary as though it is a resume—carefully written with no errors.

REFERENCES

Britton-Whitcomb, S. (2003). *Resume Magic: Trade Secrets of a Professional Resume Writer.* Indianapolis, IN: JIST Works Publishing, Inc.

Dresang, J. (2007, April 23). Liar! Liar! Won't get hired. In age of easy information, resume fibs can sabotage hunts for work. *Las Vegas Review Journal*, reprinted from *Milwaukee Journal Sentinel.*